APPLY THE LAWS IN THIS
SERIES AND EXPERIENCE

TRANSFIGURATION

Sister Thedra

Volume VI

Copyright © 2021 by Halls of Light, LLC

All rights reserved. This book or any portion thereof may not be reproduced or used in any manner whatsoever without the express written permission of the publisher except for the use of brief quotations in a book review.

ISBN: 978-1-7373071-8-1

TRANSFIGURATION

A complete change of form or appearance into a more beautiful or spiritual state. "in this light the junk undergoes a transfiguration; it shines"

The transfiguration is a sign that Jesus was to fulfill the Law and the prophets. It also assured James, Peter, and John the Jesus was indeed the Messiah.

In Christian teachings, the Transfiguration is a pivotal moment, and the setting on the mountain is presented as the point where human nature meets God: the meeting place for the temporal and the eternal, with Jesus himself as the connecting point, acting as the bridge between heaven and earth.

To the Reader

Please read and review "Divine Explanations" on page 235 for questions and definitions of terms.

This book is only a portion of the teachings and prophecies that have been given by Sananda (Jesus Christ), Sanat Kumara, and others of the higher realms, and Recorded by Sister Thedra.

Dedication

These volumes, entitled TRANSFIGURATION are dedicated to Sheryl McCartney and Kamalakar Durgapu, without whose invaluable assistance this work would not have been possible.

Contents

TO THE ONES IN HIGH PLACES 1

THE ACTION WHICH IS NOW BEING TAKEN 53

THE SLEEPERS DO NOT HEAR 107

IT SHALL BECOME PART OF THEE 153

THE MIGHTY SON KNOWN AS SANANDA 199

Mission Statement 228

Sananda's Appearance 229

About the Late Sister Thedra 230

Divine Explanations 235

Other Books by TNT Publishing 246

Esu Jesus Sananda

This reproduction is from an actual photograph taken on June 1st, 1961, in Chichen Itza, Yucatan, by one of thirty archaeologists working in the area at the time. Sananda appeared in visible, tangible body and permitted His photograph to be taken.

TO THE ONES IN HIGH PLACES

Sanat Kumara speaking:

Ye shall now give unto them this word and it shall go out unto all which are of a mind to learn ---

I say unto them that it is now come when they shall be as ones which have burned the midnite oil - and they have wasted their substance - for they have sown unto the wind -- They have been as the ones which have gathered unto themself tares and thistles -- I say they have wasted their substance - and they have not taken thot of the Father which has given unto them being -- Now I say unto them - they have given unto themself credit for being wise when they have been the greatest of fools - I say they have been fools ---

Now I say unto them which sit in high places - that there are none so foolish as the one which thinks himself wise - and none so sad as he which betrays himself or his trust -- For it is now come when the traitor shall be brot to account for his foolishness - and he shall be as one cast out - I say he shall be as one cast out -- For he has not reckoned with the law - he has not given credit where credit is due -- He has not been unto himself true - nor has he been unto his trust true -- He has been unto himself traitor - he has bartered in human sacrifice -- He has been as one which has upon his hand the blood of the saints - the blood of his children and the blood of his brother -- I say he has even sacrificed his father and mother that he be given the privilege of serving the one cast down - the dragon -- I say he shall come to know that which has held him bound hand and foot to be the dragon - which has gone the long way to bind him ---

Now I say unto thee which have a mind to learn - that there are none so sad as the one which betrays his trust - for he shall suffer the consequences - and he shall be as one cast out ---

For the first time I say unto them which betray themself - that they shall go unto a place which is prepared for them - wherein they shall begin at the beginning -- They shall have their memory blanked from them - and they shall know not that which they now boast of -- The knowledge of which they boast shall be as nought - and all their opinions shall go as the chaff before the wind ---

I speak unto them which are so minded to serve the forces of darkness -- And when ye have given of thyself that ye may be glorified and thy appetites satisfied - ye shall be as ones which have given of thy strength and of thyself that thy brother may suffer that which is unbearable -- And I say: Woe unto any man which gives unto his brother the bitter cup -- Such is my word unto thee - and ye shall study well these my words - for ye shall have cause to remember them ---

I am come that they may be delivered up which have a mind unto peace - and them which have a mind unto learning -- I shall give unto them wisdom and peace which no man shall take from them - and I am of the mind to give unto them as I have received of the Father -- Such is my inheritance - that I am one with the Father - and all the Father has is mine to give - for He has endowed unto me all that He is and all that He has -- And for this do I say:

Be ye as one prepared for to receive me and of me - for inasmuch as ye do receive me ye shall receive the Father and as ye receive Him and of Him - so shall ye receive thy Godhood -- Amen and Selah ---

I am thy older Brother - Sanat Kumara

Sister Thedra of the Emerald Cross

Handle the Keys Gently - With Wisdom

Sanat Kumara speaking unto thee which are at this altar: I say I unto thee - ye shall be as ones which have within thy hands the keys unto the place wherein I am - and I say unto thee ye shall carry them gently and with dignity -- I shall command of thee gentleness and such as is becoming of my fortunes -- I say ye have been fortuned unto me - and ye have been given unto me for a purpose – and I say ye have the power to tie my hands -- And when ye are as wayward children - I am bound to step aside - as one which shall wait for thee to grow up, to become of the age of accountability - for I have said: I give not my pearls of price unto babes who know not their worth ---

Now ye shall remember these my words and mark them well - for I am not of a mind to sibor fools -- I keep my word and I am not so minded to come into the places wherein there are ones which have upon their heads the scorpion - and upon their heart the scars which they have engraved by their own unknowing - which they CARRY AS THE ROSARIES -- I say they which do carry the scars of bygone days as something to be cherished as the ROSARY shall be as the wonton - and such are not yet ready to receive me ---

I say ye shall this day forgive thyself all thy childishness and all thy pettishness - and turn from them as ye would from the termite - - it undermines the very foundation on which ye are to build this temple.

I say that this temple shall stand - and when it is come that one is found unfit to be the foundation upon which it is builded - that block shall be removed - and I say it is the fortune of me to know wherein isanother -- So be it and Selah.

I am Sanat Kumara

Sister Thedra of the Emerald Cross

Treasure the Cup - Know It's Worth

Sanat Kumara speaking unto thee beloved Sister of the Emerald Cross Be ye as one which has my hand upon thee and ye shall be blest of me and by me -- For I say unto thee - ye shall be as one prepared for the part which shall now be given unto thee - and for this part have ye been prepared ---

Ye shall now go into all the lands of the Earth - and give unto them as ye have received - and ye shall be unto them my hand and my mouth for I shall give unto thee the gift of speech and ye shall be blest of me and by me -- And ye shall say unto them that which I shall give unto thee to say -- And I say unto thee: Great shall be thy responsibility - for I say: Great shall be the responsibility of them which have within their hand the keys unto the kingdom -- And I say the keys shall be put into thy hand - and so great shall be the responsibility that ye shall tremble within thy tracks ---

I say unto thee: Fear not for I shall be with thee unto the end - and ye shall have my hand upon thee and I shall sustain thee -- Blest shall ye be and blest shall they be which are with thee - and I say I shall give unto them that they may be sustained in their search -- And I say they shall search within themself - for within them lie the secret unto their freedom.

Be ye forever alert and mindful of thy Source - and be ye not as one which has thy hand upon the Cup - and drop it into the pit -- I say drop it not - carry it with care - and treasure it for too I say: Be ye mindful of thy treasure - let it not slip from the tips of thy fingers -- And bear this in mind - that all thy being has its beginning and its end within the Father- Mother God - and ye are but the ray sent out which shall return unto Him -- Bother not with trifles - and be ye of a mind to learn - and great shall be thy reward ---

I am thy servant and thy Brother - Sanat Kumara

Sister Thedra of the Emerald Cross

I Shall Give...Of My Own Account

Sananda speaking: -

Now it is come when ye shall be as ones which have gone the long way to bless them - and for this do I speak with thee at this time -- When ye have given of thy effort and of thy strength ye have been as ones which have chosen this part - and when ye have given of thy heart ye have done well---

And ye shall now be as ones which have my hand upon thee - for I shall bless thee and I shall give unto thee of my own account that ye may be blest - for I am now come that ye may have the part which has been kept for thee -- And ye shall be as ones which shall have thy hand in mine and ye shall be led into a place which is new unto thee - and strange shall it be - and by my hand shall ye be led -- I say ye shall be led into a place wherein ye have not been - for it is now come when ye shall be brot into a new place wherein ye have not been --

And I say - not one which ye have known has been in the place of which I speak - I say ye have not been within it - nor has any of the others ---

Now ye shall walk into this place as ones in flesh and bone and as ones prepared for a new part -- I say ye shall have a new part and ye shall be glad -- So be it and Selah -- Now ye shall be as one which have the will to learn and ye shall have many things revealed unto thee -- So be it and Selah ---

I am thy Sibor and thy Brother - Sananda

Sister Thedra of the Emerald Cross

There are No Secrets

Sanat Kumara speaking:-

Blessed one: Be ye blest of my presence - and I say unto thee ye shall be blest - for it is now come when ye shall be brot out from the place wherein ye are - into the place wherein I am - and ye shall receive of me as I have received of the Father -- So be it and Selah ---

Now I have said I am prepared to bring thee in and to give unto thee as ye are prepared to receive - and I say ye have been prepared for thy new part -- Such is thy part that ye shall give unto them as ye have received -- So be it that they too shall be blest ---

I say unto them - they too shall receive as they are prepared -- And I say - each and every one which has a mind to learn shall be given as he is capable of receiving -- Yet I say - none shall pilfer my secrets ---

I say too - there are no secrets other than thy unknowing, for when ye truly know - ye shall know and know that ye know -- And I say that none think which are wise - they k<u>no</u>w and know that they know ---

Now be ye as ones which have my hand upon thee - and I shall bless thee and I shall give unto thee as ye are capable of receiving -- Such is wisdom ---

I have set before thee the law - and ye shall study well that which is given unto thee -- Such is wisdom ---

Blest are they which cometh into this house - and blest shall ye be for having them -- I have said unto thee that none shall be turned away. So be it and Selah ---

I am Sanat Kumara

Sister Thedra of the Emerald Cross

The Reward for Obedience

Sananda speaking:-

Beloved of my being: Be ye blest of my being - for I come unto thee of the Father which has given unto me being - that ye may be blest even as I have been blest ---

Now let it be recorded even as I say it unto thee - for it shall be for the good of all mankind that which I say unto thee---

Have I not been mindful of thee and have I not given unto thee a part which has been kept for this day -- Was it not said that ye have been spared for this day that ye might fulfill thy mission in this day?

Now ye shall be as one blest - for within the time which is near ye shall walk with me and talk with me - and ye shall go and come even as I go and come -- I say ye shall go and come even as I go and come - and ye shall be as I am - for ye shall be free even as I am free -- I say ye shall be free even as I am free - for there shall be many which shall come unto thee that ye may be free -- I say many shall come unto thee for the purpose of preparing thee for the greater part -- Is it not said - this is the path of initiation - and is it not?

Now let it be recorded that there are none so foolish as the one which thinks himself wise - and none so sad as the one which betrays himself or his trust ---

And for this have I said: Be ye true unto thyself and seek ye first the Kingdom of God - and all these things shall be added unto them -- And I say that all these things are as nought in the Father's place of abode - for these things shall pass away as no-thing -- And I say that when ye have passed thru these portals ye shall be given the power and the authority to create like unto the Father - and ye shall have the wisdom and the power which is His ---

And ye shall reach out thy hand and command that which ye will and the elements shall be unto thee thy faithful and obedient servant -- They shall obey in love and harmony and ye shall create good - and ye shall be blest of God the Father for He has so willed that ye glorify Him in the Earth -- And I say - for this has many been sent unto thee that this may be accomplished -- Amen -- So be it and Selah ---

Give unto the Father all the credit and all the praise now and evermore -- So be it and Selah ---

I am thy Brother and thy Sibor - Sananda Son of God -- Amen - So be it --

Sister Thedra of the Emerald Cross

The Rod Which Shall Become Brass

Sanat Kumara speaking: -

This day I would give unto thee one commandment: Be ye as ones which have within thy hand the rod which shall become brass ---

I say: Within thy hand is the key unto the place wherein the Father abides ---

Be ye as ones which can comprehend that which I have said unto thee ---

I say: Ye shall be as ones which have the mind to walk in the way set before thee - ye shall turn from thy childishness and ye shall grow into maturity ---

Ye shall put away thy small ways and ye shall be as adults which have upon thy heads the Crown of the Sun - and ye shall walk which way it tilts not ---

I say: Ye shall now walk as ones which have within thy hands a lamp which has been lit within a dark place - and I say ye shall carry that lamp high - and ye shall be custodians of it -- Ye shall guard it well and watch that an ill wind does not extinguish it ---

I say: Ye have been made custodian of the lamp which flickers dimly in a dark place - and ye shall feed that flame from thy own oil - I say from thy own oil shall ye feed it ---

Ye shall give thy attention unto this which I say unto thee: Ye shall practice that which I give unto thee -- Ye shall not turn from the way set before thee - I say woe unto any man which turneth back ---

I have given unto thee commandments which ye have not lived to the fullest - and ye shall this day begin thy search for the key which lies within these commandments - and ye shall be as one which has betrayed himself when ye pass them by lightly ---

I say: Ye shall turn back each and every page and find them one by one - and practice them until they become thy very nature -- I say this is thy key into the secret place of the Most High Living God - for none enter into His place of abode unprepared -- So be it that He has accepted thee - yet ye shall not enter unprepared ---

Too I say: This is the day of preparation - and I say all within the place wherein I am have come that ye may be brot in -- Yet ye and ye alone shall prepare thyself - and when ye are so prepared one shall come unto thee and give unto thee as ye are prepared to receive ---

I say we are not so foolish as to give of our pearls unto babes who know not their worth ---

I say: When ye grow to maturity - and when ye become accountable for all thy actions - one shall come unto thee and give unto thee as ye are prepared to receive - no more - no less ---

I am thy older Brother - Sanat Kumara

Sister Thedra of the Emerald Cross

Prepare for the Great Learning

Sanat Kumara speaking unto thee - beloved ones which have remembered this hour -- Have ye not remembered it for thy own sake? Have ye not been unto thyself true for this moment? I see thee as ones laboring late and with weary hands for the sake of others that they may know that which is given unto thee ---

Ye shall now say unto them in my name - that they which are of a mind to learn shall be as ones prepared for the great learning - for it is now come when I shall speak thru the ones which have prepared themself for this part -- I shall be as one which has the power and the authority to give unto them such gifts as speech - hearing and writing - I shall withhold that of sight for the time - for it is the better part of wisdom ---

Now say unto them that when it is come that they are given such gifts as hearing and speaking and writing - they shall be as ones which have great responsibility - for I say - great shall be the responsibility of anyone whichsoever that takes up the banner of Truth - for I say the truth shall be as the pearl without price - I say that they dive deep for the pearl without price - I say that they pay for every pearl -- Yet I say: Ye cannot buy with thy puny coin this pearl of which I speak for it is truly without price ---

Therefore I guard it well - I treasure my heritage - I am not a fool! I waste not my substance nor my inheritance which the Father has willed unto me - I say - they which do are fools indeed ---

Now I say that they which do receive such gifts shall abide by the law of Love - Truth and Justice -- They shall walk in the Light of the Christ and turn not to the left nor to the right -- They shall be responsible for their actions and for that which they send out -- They shall be as ones on whose shoulders rest the responsibility of all their words and all their deeds -- And I say: Woe unto anyone whichsoever who puts words into my mouth ---

I have seen this done and I say I spew them out -- I say: I am not about to be given the bitter cup -- I am not easily prompted to offense yet I say they do offend me - and my love alone keeps me from saying that which ye would say -- Yet I am mindful of their weakness and of their unknowing - Yet I say that when they are confronted with their foolishness they shall be as ones plagued by it - they shall be as ones brot up short -- I say they shall come to know that which they have done and they shall be held accountable for their foolishness So be it and Selah ---

Now I say unto thee my hand made manifest: Ye shall send this out and I say: The seed planted in fertile soil shall grow as the banyan tree and great shall be the harvest thereof I say ye shall be blest of me and by me - and ye shall sign all these documents thusly:

Sister Thedra of the Emerald Cross

Revelation is a Gift of God

Sanat Kumara speaking: -

Blest art thou and blest shall ye be - for I am come that ye may be blest -- Now ye shall see that which shall be given unto thee to see - and ye shall recognize it for what it is -- I say: Ye shall now see that which shall be shown thee thru revelation -- I say many things shall be revealed unto thee - and ye shall know - and know that ye know ---

Be ye as one prepared for such revelation -- I say: Ye shall have many things revealed unto thee - and ye shall be as ones which have prepared thyself for such revelation -- It is said that revelation is a gift of God the Father - given unto thee as part of thy inheritance - so it is - And so be it a great gift indeed - yet I say unto thee - wisdom is the greatest of all -- So be it when ye have become wise - ye shall be able to control the elements - and ye shall go out from the Earth as one unbound - and ye shall have free concourse into all the planets of the galaxy - and ye shall move freely without any apparatus other than that which ye create from the virgin eth - and ye shall be as one in full command -- Ye shall create from the virgin eth - and ye shall need no machinery - no gadgets - ye shall be master of the elements - ye shall command them and they shall obey thee in love - peace and harmony.

This has been given unto the Sons of God as part of their inheritance I say - when ye are brot before the Great White Altar wherein I am - ye shall be as one which has prepared thyself for this part -- Ye shall stand before this Altar and I shall declare for thee thy freedom - and ye shall be as one freed from all bondage - forever free: ---

Blest are they which do receive their freedom for they shall see God. So be it the will of God the Father ---

Now ye shall send this out that they may bear witness of these my words - for it is as my words made manifest unto thee - and as they prepare themself - so shall they receive ---

It is said that when one stands upon the Holy Ground wherein stands the Altar of White Alabaster that they are never the same - so be it a truth -- Yet I say - some do wait for yet another day - and some do become overly anxious - and they do become sick at heart and fall - and become bruised -- And they are not to be censored - for they are but the ones which would rush in where angels fear to tread -- I say - they who try to storm the gates of the temple are foolish indeed - for they find it not -- Is it not said that he which comes any other way is a liar and a thief? I say he is not permitted to enter these portals without the proper credentials. And I am the gate keeper - and I watch with diligence that none pilfer the secrets which shall be revealed unto the just and the worthy ---

I am not in lethargy nor am I a fool - I keep watch over my own - I do not sacrifice my own - I do know them and I guard them by day and by night -- Yet I say - be ye as ones prepared for the greater part - for this is thy inheritance in full So be it and Selah ---

I am come that ye may be brot out this day -- So be it I am glad it is come when I may come in and counsel with thee and speak with thee thusly -- So be it I shall speak with thee when ye are prepared to receive me ---

Yet I shall say: Woe unto anyone whichsoever who puts words into my mouth - for I shall spew them out and great shall be thy sorrow ---

I am within the place wherein I am prepared for this day and none shall take from me the word - nor add unto ---

I am thy Sibor and thy Brother - Sanat Kumara

Sister Thedra of the Emerald Cross

With My Presence I Bless Them

Sanat Kumara speaking: -

Blest art thou my child - and blest shall they be which read these my words -- For this shall I give them unto thee - that they may receive them thru thee -- Such is my hand made manifest unto them ---

Now say unto them as I would - that with my being I bless them - and with my presence I bless them ---

I say: Because I am - I do bless them - and for this do I speak unto thee my Sister of the Emerald Cross - that they too may come to know me - and that they too may be prepared to receive me and of me -- For it is now come when I shall manifest in physical - for the purpose of giving unto the world that for which they have waited ---

I say I have waited long for this day when I shall speak thusly -- And it is now come when I shall come unto thee in flesh and bone - and I shall counsel thee as one of thy own* I say ye shall be as one prepared to receive me - for I say - I am now prepared to come unto thee as one of thy own - for this have ye waited -- Now ye shall receive me and of me - and ye shall be glad for thy preparation -- So be it and Selah.

Now ye shall say unto them - that when they are sufficiently prepared -I shall come unto them and I shall counsel them and I shall give unto them a gift far more precious than frankincense and myrrh.

*As mortal man

Now I say: One shall come unto thee from out the place wherein I am - and he shall be unto thee thy hand and thy foot - I say he shall be unto thee all that the Father would have him be -- And he shall bless thee and he shall give unto thee that which is wise and prudent -- So be it and Selah ---

Blest are they which come in the name of the Father - Son and Holy Ghost ---

I say I shall send one out from the place wherein I am as one prepared to give unto thee that which the Father would have him give unto thee - and ye shall be glad to receive him and it shall profit thee much ---

I am with thee that the Father's will might be done in us and thru us. So be it we shall glorify Him with the Earth - Hallelujah

Sister Thedra of the Emerald Cross

Blest are They Which Learn This Lesson

Sananda speaking: -

Beloved of my being: I speak after my beloved Brother Sanat Kumara - for the purpose which has been withheld for this time -- I have not spoken for a short time - now I too shall open my mouth - and I shall say unto thee that which is prompted by love - wisdom and mercy -- I have come at this moment that ye may be blest - and too I say the others shall be blest - for have they too not come unto this altar that they might receive their part? I say they too shall be blest -- Too I say: All which take within their heart these my words - shall be blest of me and by me -- I say - they which open up their heart I shall touch them and they shall receive me unto themself - I say - they shall receive me unto themself ---

Now for this do I speak unto thee - that they may come to know me by my new name - for I say it is now the new day - the new age - when the old shall pass away and all things shall be made new - I say all things shall be made new ---

And ye shall remember these my words for ye shall have cause to remember them -- When ye have remembered them ye shall look deep within thyself and search out that which lies within the secret place - and ye shall rid thyself of all that which is unto thyself the gross of which ye have garnered unto thyself - which is thy legirons - and unto thee thy own pitfalls -- I say - all the pitfalls are within thy own self.

I say: Cleanse thy place of abode - cleanse thy place of abode and prepare thyself for the greater part ---

Wherein is it said that there is none so sad as the one which betrays himself -- I speak unto thee from the depth of my very being - I cry aloud unto the Father that He may give unto me of His Grace - that ye may be delivered out ---

I say ye have slept overtime - and I now give unto thee a key - and ye have but to turn it within the gate -- For I say ye shall pass from the pore into the Holy Christ body as one made new - as one made whole as one purified - when ye have learned the law which governs thy being. I say the key is but this: Love thy life which the Father has endowed unto thee - and thy freedom is assured thee ---

Blest are they which learn this lesson -- Fortune unto thyself such love - and I say ye shall stand free even as I am free

I bless thee and I give unto the Father thanks that He has allowed me the privilege of coming unto thee - so be it I shall praise Him forever. Amen and Selah ---

I am He which was born of Mary and the ward of Joseph called Jesus the Christ - known within this temple as Sananda Son of God -- So be it and Selah ---

Sister Thedra of the Emerald Cross

The Wordless Ceremonies

He which is without sound speaketh:-

Ceboleth Cobola Cabota and blessings upon thee my child -- I come unto thee from out the silence - I come unto thee from out the silence that all men may know that which I know ---

I say that upon this day - and within this thy year of 1962 I have come unto thee from out the silence wherein I have performed many ceremonies without words -- I say my work is without words - for I am the Master of Vibration which is soundless -- I move without sound - I am motion - I create by motion - within motion I create -- I move - I create - I create as I move -- I go out without sound - I am soundless -- I am movement - I go in with no sound - I go out without sound - I go out from the great void wherein is no sound -- I move upon the eth - I go into the depth wherein is no sound - I move and there becomes sound.

I am he which creates from the depth of silence - I bring forth - I go into the great void wherein is no thing and I move and there becomes.

I cause that which shall be - to become -- I call forth from the depth of my being all which becomes -- I call forth that which shall become worlds without end -- I call forth that which I will - and I give unto it vibration - and NOTHING goes out from me without first having form. I say nothing goes out from me without first having form.

I call forth form - and from myself I give it vibration - and then it becomes that which is heard and seen -- I say it first takes form - then it is heard and seen within thy own dimension -- I say - first it becomes form within my realm and then it is seen and heard - and felt within thy realm ---

I speak unto thee from out the silence - I speak without sound - yet ye have heard me and recorded these my words that they which have ears to hear may hear them -- I say that they have heard NOthing with their physical ears - for it is as nothing -- I say they are as ones deaf - for they hear NOT with their physical ears ---

Be ye blest for this my word unto them thru thee - I say I shall give unto thee a gift and by that gift shall ye be known

I am the one which has opened this door that this part may be added unto the others - and this shall go out with that of the others of Sanat Kumara and Sananda - and ye shall say I am He which is without sound. And I AM and I AM

Sister Thedra of the Emerald Cross

It is Not Wise to Change One Word --Take Heed --

Sanat Kumara speaking:-

Now my beloved - in the day which is now come ye shall take up thy pen as one which has upon thy head a crown - and ye shall be given a part which shall be for the good of all mankind -- And ye shall record that which is said unto thee - and I command thee give it unto <u>them</u> as it is spoken - for not one word shall be misplaced or mis-spoken -- I say it shall reach the ones for which they are intended - for it shall be given from the Hiarchi (Hierarchy) - and it shall not be necessary to change it*-- I say it shall reach the ones which are willing to receive it - and it is in no wise the better part of wisdom to change one word --

Was it not given unto the foolish to change the words of the Scriptures many times? Have they not lost their essence and have they not lost the word**- and have they not given unto themself credit for being wise?

* This document

** The people have lost the Word

Now when ye have finished with this part ye shall give unto them permission to go*** - and ye shall prepare thyself for the part which shall be given unto thee as a part separate -- And yet it shall go out unto them with this - for this shall prepare <u>them</u> which are prepared to receive this new part which shall be brot forth this day ---

Now ye shall give unto them the new part as it is spoken and ye shall be as one which has my hand upon thee -- And I say: Woe unto any man which points a finger at thee -- I now speak unto thee my recorder - known unto us here within this Temple as Sister Thedra of the Emerald Cross: Blest shall ye be for I shall bless thee with my presence and with my very being shall I bless thee by day and by night. So be it and Selah ---

Blest are they which have come into this place wherein ye are and blest shall they be ---

I am thy older brother and thy Sibor - Sanat Kumara

Sister Thedra of the Emerald Cross

*** From this altar

The Vine & The Root

Eternal Mother am I -- I am one which has given of my being that ye may have thy being -- I am separated from thee and I am not afar - for I am thee and thou art me -- Blest art thou for I am blest - and I am that which blesses and I am that which is blest -- As my hands bless my feet I bless thee my child -- I bless thee from the center of my being - which ye are which have gone out from me as the vine from its root -- I send unto thee the vine - life - and I sustain thee from the root which I am -- I AM and I know that I AM and I am glad.

I say: Arise O my child and come unto me - thy Eternal Mother - and I shall give unto thee that which I have kept for thee -- I say ye have waited long for thy inheritance which ye forfeited long ago -

Be ye as one which has my love - and my heart shall encompass thee in thy journey home -- I say it is now come when ye shall be brot home as one free - forever free -- And therein is cause for great joy - so be it the music shall ring out thru all the cosmos - and they shall hear it and they shall see that which is given unto them to see -- Yet they shall be in no wise - wise - for they shall be as the sleepers - for they shall believe that which they see to be illusions of their own puny mind - they shall think that they are dreaming - and is it not so?

Now I say - the sleepers shall sleep on - while the ones which are awakened shall ascend unto me even as the Sons of God have returned unto me -- I say the day of the new dispensation is come when they shall see that which is done openly - and they shall not know that which they see - for they shall be as ones walking in their sleep -- I say they which are awake shall be brot out of bondage this day -- I say it is now come when one shall be sent from out the temple wherein stands the

Altar of White Alabaster - which shall bring thee into the place wherein there shall stand a light which is LIVING LIGHT - it is Life itself - it is undistinguishable and it is not a power of Earth -- It is the Life force and that Flame is the force from which cometh all fire - all warmth -- And Love is the feeling quality - and that which motivates the Love Principle ---

I am the Love Principle in action -- I AM and I know myself to be Love in action -- I am love and I am action - and because I am thou art and LOVE motivates thy every action and for this do I now make myself known unto thee - for this is my part with thee - to prepare thee for thy new part -- And I have spoken unto thee many times and for this do ye now receive me and give unto me credit for that which I am.

Have ye not walked within the Temple of Fire? Have ye not walked upon the flame wherein ye were unharmed? I say ye have been blest - yea even purified -- Blest are they which have entered upon the steps of the Flame Temple wherein ye shall go -- Blest am I to receive thee.

I shall say unto them that which ye will not - for it is given unto me to know the wisdom thereof -- I am within the place wherein I abide as the Son - or the Central Sun - from which ye have gone out - and I am within this place prepared to receive thee -- Such is my joy - and my great love shall enfold thee in thy preparation -- I bless thee O my child. Bring thyself unto this altar at a later hour and I shall speak with thee again this day ---

Sister Thedra of the Emerald Cross

The Seal of Solomon

And for this do I bring thee unto this altar -- Bless thee my soul - be ye as one come out from me - and be ye as one which has returned unto me -- Go NOT out from me - and I shall make of thee a prophet in thy own right ---

I shall bring thee back unto me from whence ye have gone out - and therein I shall prepare a part for thee - and ye shall walk with dignity - and upon thy head shall be the Crown of the Sun - and upon thy forehead the Seal of Solomon -- And ye shall know as I know - for ye shall be one with me and I say - ye shall return unto me in honor and with dignity - for such is the nature of my Sons which return unto me - And ye shall walk with me and ye shall talk with me and ye shall know thyself to be as I - and I shall give unto thee all that I am - for I am thee and thou art me -- Such is my part - to bring thee back from whence ye went out - and I say ye shall go out no more -- So be it I am glad ---

I am thy eternal Mother -- So be it and Selah ---

I am known as Sara Mother of Abraham -

Sister Thedra of the Emerald Cross

The Purpose

Sanat Kumara speaking: -

Blest art thou and blest shall ye be -- I say ye have come together for the purpose of bringing about order from out the chaos -- And ye have been as ones working blindly - for ye have walked step at a time knowing not that which is ahead of thee -- I say ye shall be as ones blest of me and by me - yet ye shall walk in the way set before thee ---

Ye shall have upon thy shoulders the full responsibility of thy own progress -- Ye shall apply thyself whole heartedly - and ye shall not let any word of slander pass from thy lips -- Ye shall blame not one which is among thee for their unknowing -- Ye shall be as one responsible for every word which passes from thy lips - ye shall be held accountable for all thy words -- And I say - they shall return unto thee multiplied a thousand fold - for this do I speak unto thee thusly ---

For I say - ye shall be as one cursed of thy own words - or ye shall be as one blest by them -- I say ye shall count to ten before ye say one word of which ye are not sure -- Ask of thyself: "Is this prompted by LOVE - PEACE AND HARMONY?"---

I say it is the better part of wisdom to see the Light of the Christ and to turn from thy petty way - thy little way - and I shall counsel thee in greater things -- So be it and Selah ---

Bless thee O my soul - I am come that ye may be blest -- Amen -- So be it and Selah ---

I am Sanat Kumara

Sister Thedra of the Emerald Cross

Time of Initiation for the Earth & Man

Sanat Kumara speaking: -

Blest art thou and blest shall ye be - and for this do I come that ye may be blest ---

I am One which has guided and guarded thee - and I have watched thee struggle within the mire of the Earth while she has gone thru her many initiations -- For has she not also gone thru many - and have ye not likewise been with her?

Now I say - ye shall stand with her thru this - her (the Earth) time of initiation - for she is going thru a great and trying time of crisis so to speak -- I say - now - this moment. She is being held within our hand as a baby which is being lifted from the womb by Caesarean birth -- I say she - the Earth is being re-born - and we thy guardians are responsible for her safety ---

And I say - each of us has been given certain responsibilities - certain parts - and for this have we been prepared -- Now I say - ye shall stand with us as ones which has upon thy shoulders certain responsibilities - and ye shall forget them NOT - for this is the day of action - "Preparation"!!-- Days for the great revelation are now at hand. I say that the foolish shall say 'I am being prepared' - for I say <u>ye</u> are preparing thyself - none other prepare thee -- I say - when ye have given thy whole heart - thy whole self to thy preparation - one shall come unto thee and give unto thee that for which ye have prepared thyself for to receive --

Now I say - ye shall be as ones alert - for too I say: Ye shall be as one on whose shoulders rest the responsibility of thy brothers and thy sisters -- Yet ye are not to be held accountable for their shortcomings or for their part -- Ye shall be mindful of thy own attitude - of thy tongue - of thy appearances -- Ye shall walk as the living example of an initiate - and ye are to remember at ALL TIMES why ye have come unto this place ---

I say - woe unto anyone who-so-ever which speaks lightly of this endeavor - for the law is sure and swift -- And I say it is a law - that anyone - whosoever he be - which says as much as shall besmirch the sisters or the brothers shall pay for such foolishness ---

Blest are they which walk in the way set before them ---

Now I say unto thee: Ye have come together again for the purpose of learning the laws which have hitherto been hidden from thee -- And I now say unto thee - when ye have learned this lesson well - I shall reveal the next one unto thee ---

Be ye alert and wise and I shall be unto thee Sibor - and I shall counsel thee in the way of the wise - and I shall bless thee as I have been blest -- Amen and Selah ---

I am thy older Brother - Sanat Kumara

Sister Thedra of the Emerald Cross

The Father has Set Up This Altar

Sanat Kumara speaking: -

Beloved ones which have come unto this altar which the Father has set up - I say unto thee: I am now prepared to give unto thee as ye are prepared to receive -- I say when ye are so prepared - I shall come unto thee and I shall counsel thee in wisdom and in love ---

I say ye shall prepare thyself - for as ye prepare thyself - so shall ye receive -- I say ye shall be unto thyself true and follow in the way set before thee ---

Now it is come when there shall be great stress upon the Earth and within the Earth -- For I say unto thee my beloved ones which are now within this temple - that as sure as ye are here before me - ye shall stand and bear witness of my words that the forces which have been built up within the Earth and about the Earth shall break forth as with a mighty blast -- I say - that within the twinkling of an eye - the force which has built up in and about the Earth shall give forth with one mighty blast - and it shall be for the reason that the traitors have willed it so ---

I say that when they have gone the long way to serve the dragon they have betrayed themself -- And too I say - ye which now sit within this place which I have caused to be brot into manifestation - has the PEACE and the COMPREHENSION of me and that which I say unto thee -- Ye shall give more attention unto thy part - and ye shall be as ones alert unto thy part which has been given unto thee because ye have asked for this part -- I say - of thy own choice have ye been given this part - I say ye have volunteered for this part - and ye have forgotten thy choosing -- Such is the pity of thy memory being blanked from thee - I say the pity of it is the blanking of thy memory - and too I say - ye which will it so - shall have it restored ---

Now if ye so will it ye shall be as ones given a new part - and for this have ye been brot into this place -- And in the time which is near one shall come into this place which has the power and the authority to give unto thee great and wise <u>instructions</u> - and ye shall be wise indeed to follow them ---

I say ye shall not be opinionated nor shall ye be deceived, for I have given unto my hand made manifest - the word which shall be unto her the key -- I say she shall know him - and ye shall be as one wise indeed to hear that which she says unto thee - for I have sibored her wisely -- Such is my word unto thee ---

I say - go from this altar filled with joy and love -- I say I shall bless thee with my being ---

I am thy older Brother - Sanat Kumara

Sister Thedra of the Emerald Cross

I Know Where Thy Strength Lies

Sanat Kumara speaking: -

Sanda speaks unto thee from out the silence -- Be ye blest by her presence - for she speaks out the fullness of her heart for that purpose - I say ye shall be blest by her and of her being -- Ye shall record for them that which she shall say unto thee and they shall bear witness of her words unto thee.

Be ye as one filled with compassion for him which has gone from this altar - for he is now given unto much sorrow and torment -- I say he has gone from this altar of his own free will and by his own choice has he gone - yet he has upon his own shoulders the responsibility of his own free will -- For the first time it is said unto thee: He shall return. So be it and Selah

I am with thee unto the end -- So be it and Selah -- Ye shall go and do that which shall be done ---

Now ye shall give unto them these words of the beloved Sanda - and she shall say unto them that which shall bless them--

Sanda

Beloved of my being: I come from out the silence that ye may be blest. Be ye aware of me and these my words - for they shall be a link between us -- Ye shall come to know me as I know thee - I say ye shall come to know me and I shall counsel thee - for it is given unto me to be the complement of our beloved Sanat Kumara -- I am known by many names yet I say ye shall know me by this name ---

I have given unto thee this name for a purpose which shall serve thee well -- Ye shall remember me in the days to come for I shall come unto thee in the days of stress - and for this am I prepared ---

Now for the first time I speak unto thee thru this temple and at this altar- and I say unto thee in wisdom and with great love - that ye have been brot together for the purpose which ye as yet do not know ---

Ye are as yet following in darkness - ye walk one step at a time -- And I say unto thee my beloved ones: Ye do not walk alone - for many times my hand is upon thee in loving silence -- I see thy tears of joy and of disappointment - I see thy struggles - I know thy poultices - and I know where thy strength lies-- I say ye shall come to know as I know and ye shall be glad for thy knowing ---

Wherein is it said that there shall be one sent from out the temple wherein stands the Great White Altar - to help thee in thy struggle - and to give unto thee the plan which as yet has not been fully revealed unto thee -- I say - blest are they which do endure ---

I am come that my light may bless and sustain thee -- I say unto thee ye shall have within thee the fortitude to endure and be ye mindful of thy Benefactors and of thy own divinity.

Walk as the Son of God the Father - and I shall give unto thee a part and ye shall be glad ---

I am thy older sister and thy Sibor - Sanda

Sister Thedra of the Emerald Cross

Praise...
Song of Solomon

Tarman of Allecea speaking: -

Blest art thou - blest shall ye be- and be it so and so be it. I am with thee and I shall be with thee unto the end ---

Be ye as one which has my hand upon thee -- O my Soul be thou blest by the Father-Mother God - I AM - and I am forever and eternally one with thee -- O my Soul - praise Him forever and forevermore -- I come unto thee that ye may be blest as I have been blest ---

I say unto thee - ye shall receive of God the Father as I have received - and give unto Him all the praise and the glory forever and forever -- Allejulia -- Praise His Holy Name ---

Blest art they which come unto the altar which has been set up in His name and blest shall they be ---

And now it is come when ye shall sing the Songs of Solomon for I shall bless thee with my being - and I shall give unto thee the gift of Solomon - I shall adorn thy head with pearls and rubies - and sapphires shall I give unto thee - I shall give unto thee the sardonyx for thy breastplate - I shall give unto thee a ring for thy hand - and in it shall be a planet and it shall be called fortune of the Sons of God - and on it shall be written these words:

And therein is the symphony of the spheres - Be ye blest O my Soul for I have sung unto thee my song in holy adoration -

And ye shall give it unto them that they may bear witness. One shall set it to music and it shall glorify the Father -- So be it and Selah.

I am thy Sibor and thy older Brother - Tarman of Allecea

Sister Thedra of the Emerald Cross

Commandments: - Change No Word

Sananda speaking: -

Beloved of my being: Ye come unto this altar this morning that ye may be given light and in abundance -- I say ye shall have it - and ye shall glorify the Father in the Earth and ye shall be unto Him his mouth for ye shall say the words which He shall put into thy mouth - and ye shall be unto Him His hand made manifest unto them -- For He shall give unto thee the power and the authority to write that which He has for them - and ye shall <u>change</u> no <u>word</u> - for it is the greatest of folly.

I say <u>not</u> <u>one</u> <u>word</u> shall be changed -- So be it there is a law governing such things -- Ye have been commanded obedience in all things and ye have kept the commandments given thee -- Ye have made haste to obey and I am glad - for it is the better part of wisdom -- May the Father see fit to give unto <u>them</u> the same comprehension ---

I say - they which ask of Him shall have comprehension - yet they shall learn to prepare themself for such as He has willed unto them ---

I say great are their legirons - which are the things they fortune unto themself - such as their karma - their opinions - their wonton -- Their very rebelliousness is sufficient to keep them short of their course ---

Blest are they which turn from their own wonton way -- And they which do turn unto the Source of their being for Light shall be as ones blest forevermore - they shall see God face to face -- So be it and Selah.

When they do turn from their own wonton way they shall have their legirons cut away - they shall be blest forevermore. They shall find Peace such as they have not known ---

I come not to bring peace - but to make way for peace -- I give not unto the wonton - I give unto the ones which prepare themself to receive me -- I ask of them only their will to learn and their hand - that I might lead them out of bondage. I lead gently - yet I demand of them: "Pick up thy feet! And walk - drag not thy feet"!

For I am not the burro - ye ride <u>not</u> my back! Ye are created in the image of God the Father - and ye are commanded:

"Let thy own Light shine"

"Let thy own Light shine"

"Let thy own Light shine"

And I am one sent of God the Father that ye may find thy way home. I am <u>one</u> of the Wayshowers ---

And I have been called by many names - yet in this new day - this new dispensation - I return unto them which have heard my voice and invited me in - as Sananda ---

Yet there are many which deny me by any name -- I say it is now come when they which are prepared to receive me and of me - shall come to know me as Sananda - Son of God. I come as such - I shall go as such - and I would that all which are upon the Earth today might go as I go -- Yet I have said that I have come that my covenant might be fulfilled with the Father and with thee ---

And some shall go into their new places of abode knowing not that I have ever come into the Earth as man - and they are the ones which shall not know that there is a place prepared for them ---

I say that there are yet others which call themself CHRISTIAN which shall go into their new places denying that I am come - and that I am the Son of God - and that I am not as yet come -- They shall deny me and these my words - and I say unto thee: These are the ANTICHRISTS - spoken of in thy Scriptures ---

I say they are the ANTI-CHRISTS - spoken of in thy Scriptures ---

I say be ye alert - and be ye aware of them - for they lay for thee many a snare ---

Blest are they which hold fast - for I shall be with them unto the end - and I am thy Sibor and thy Brother ---

For thy sake have I spoken unto them - and ye shall give unto them as ye have received ---

I am Sananda - once known as Jesus Christ - born of Mary - and the ward of Joseph – Blest are they -- Amen and Selah.

Sister Thedra of the Emerald Cross

Ye are in Me
Solen Aum Solen

Father Solen speaking; -

Behold ME - I AM - and I AM and shall ever BE ---

I AM GOD -- I AM HE WHICH IS and which SHALL EVER BE.

Behold ME - Because I AM - thou art -- Behold ME in all that ye are - and I have given unto thee being -- And because I AM thou art -- Behold ME - and give unto ME credit for being that which I AM - and give unto thyself credit for being MY SON - MY SON ---

For I have given of Myself that ye may have being - and because ye are in ME and have thy being in ME - ye are of ME and ye ARE ME. Behold ME and give unto thyself credit for being a Son of God thy Father ---

I say - rejoice this day that ye have received thy Sonship which I have willed unto thee ---

Behold my handiwork and rejoice -- Rejoice forevermore for I say unto thee ye shall see ME face to face - Hallelujah - Amen ---

Say I unto thee: Ye shall return unto ME even as ye went out - perfect in all things - and I say ye shall behold ME face to face -- I say for this shall ye rejoice forevermore - Hallelujah ---

Blest are they which return unto ME this day -- I say unto thee my child - blest are they which return this day ---

Blest are MY SONS -- Amen and Selah ---

I AM thy Father Solen

So be it and be it so --

Sister Thedra of the Emerald Cross

False "Masters" vs The True Master

Sanat Kumara speaking: -

Beloved of my being: I come unto thee this morning that they may receive of me as ye have received -- I say ye have received of me and by me - yet they have not touched the sleeve of my garment - for they have been as ones asleep -- They stir slightly and they are yet dreaming while others are dead upon their feet!

I say that the dead walk among thee - they are as ones motivated and animated by the astral world - they know not! They "think" and they give unto themself credit for being wise - when they are fools indeed - for they are not the ones they believe themself to be!---

They have wandered long in darkness and they have not the will to awaken -- T<u>hey</u> have thot themself wise and t<u>hey</u> give unto themself great and impressive titles and degrees dictated of man - and because of these things they call themself "Master"

I ask of thee: Are they? Wherein can they heal the sick? Wherein can they add one cubit unto their height? Wherein can they stay the elements? Wherein can they give sight unto the blind - or wherein can they give unto the dying comfort?

Answer them the questions which they ask of thee when they come and give unto them no proof - for I say unto thee they shall come and they shall demand proof - yet I say - give unto them NONE! -- For it shall be given unto the ones which are prepared and unto none other - and I say the one so prepared de<u>man</u>ds NO proof - and the one which is not prepared shall have it NOT!

Blest are they which do receive proof - for he has prepared himself to receive it ---

I am come that he might have it ---

Blest art thou my hand made manifest - for ye shall see me face to face ---

I AM - and I am forever one with the Father which has caused me to be -- Amen -- So be it and Selah ---

I am Sanat Kumara

Sister Thedra of the Emerald Cross

The Painful Awakening

Sananda speaking: -

Beloved of my being: Go into all the lands of the Earth and say unto them these words -- Blest shall they be which receive them and blest shall ye be -- Blest are my servants for I shall glorify them even as the Father has glorified Himself in me -- Such is my word unto thee ---

Now say unto them as I would and in my name - that they shall awaken! For it is now time that they arise and come forth, I say they shall awaken!

And too I say - they shall have great pains in the process for I say they have fortuned unto themself much unrest while they have slept -- And they shall be as ones rudely awakened and they shall wonder why they have slept so late -- I say it is later than they know - for the time is NOW and NOW is the time ---

I say this is the time which has been spoken of in the Scriptures - for it is the Battle of Armageddon - when the forces of darkness have within their hand the power to destroy thy planet Earth -- And I say that they shall be staid even at the cost of much sorrow -- I say sorrow there shall be and too I say - all which are so minded to walk in the way set before them shall be brot out of bondage - and they shall be as ones which are prepared for their deliverance from the torment which shall come upon the Earth - and unto the ones which are traitors unto themself ---

I say - woe is he which does betray himself - and woe shall he be which gives unto his brother the bitter cup ---

Blest are they which give unto me credit for being that which I am.

And I come that they may have Light -- Such is my mission at this time.

I am with thee that they may come to know me even as ye know me. So be it and Selah ---

I am thy Sibor and thy Brother - Sananda

Sister Thedra of the Emerald Cross

None Shall Go Unnoticed

Sanat Kumara speaking: -

Blest are they which come unto this altar for the purpose of learning of the Father - Son and Holy Ghost - for I say unto thee my children: Ye shall be blest even as we are blest which are within the place wherein I am ---

I say: unto this place ye shall come and ye shall know as we know, for I say none shall go unnoticed, for it is the law. When one is prepared for such learning, he is found and brot in - and for this are we prepared. I say we are prepared for this day when there shall be a great gathering in - and there shall be great joy and much gladness -- For ye shall come to know of which I speak - for I have said: blest are they which come into the place wherein I am, and I am within this place for the purpose of bringing thee in-- So be it and Selah

Blest are they which come - for they shall receive of me as I have received of the Father - Son and Holy Ghost -- Amen and Selah ---

I am Sanat Kumara

Sister Thedra of the Emerald Cross

I Have Other Hands & Mouths

Sanat Kumara speaking: -

Beloved of my being: In this day shall ye be brot out of bondage - and ye shall be as one prepared to deliver them out for this do I now come unto thee ---

I have sent one out of the place wherein I am that ye may have Light. I have given unto him the power and the authority to give unto thee all that is necessary unto thee. I say he is now prepared for his part. When ye have received him and of him, great shall be thy work and ye shall be blest. Ye shall be blest and ye shall know that which ye are to do. So be it such as ye have waited for ---

I am now prepared for my part - now ye shall be prepared for that which ye are to do - Let it be recorded that ye shall be prepared that ye might give unto them that which shall be unto them their salvation. I say ye shall be as my hand and as my mouth made manifest unto them.

And too I say - I have other hands and other mouths ---

I say I shall cause them to be raised up and prepared for this part - for there is much to be done - and I have said that there is little time before I shall come into the world in physical form - even as I have come unto thee - I say even as I have come unto thee -- I say too - even as my Brother and Christed Sananda has come unto thee that ye may have this part - for ye have asked that ye might be lifted up - ye have given of thyself that this might be accomplished ---

Bless them which do come and are lifted up - blest shall they be.

Blest am I that I might come unto thee - for do I not know thee and remember thee before ye went out into darkness wherein ye forgot me? So be it ye shall return and I am glad. So be it and Selah --- -

I am Sanat Kumara

Sister Thedra of the Emerald Cross

The Great Drama

Sanat Kumara speaking: -

Now it is come when ye shall see me face to face and I am glad -- I say ye shall now see me face to face - and for this shall ye be prepared and ye shall be glad for thy preparation - for I say unto thee - ye are as ones which shall be unto the world great light -- Ye know not the part which ye are now given -- Ye are as ones playing thy part upon a darkened stage - neither do ye know that ye are the director of thy part.

I have said unto thee: "Ye write thy own passport into the place of my abode" - it is so and so be it - for it is the law that ye prepare thyself for thy parts which ye play - that which is given unto thee to do ---

And now it is come when ye shall be called out of thy bed at the midnight hour and ye shall answer that call - and ye shall be as ones which have prepared thyself in silence -- Ye boast not of thy accomplishments - nor of thy greatness - nor of thy wisdom - ye walk as the initiate -- Ye go in and out among them as one of them - yet ye give not the bitter cup - nor do ye take part in their frivolity -- Ye give no offense or take no offense -- Ye look unto no man for thy salvation and ye give unto the Father credit for thy being - and unto thy Benefactors credit for thy <u>well-being</u> -- And ye give unto no man that which is given unto thee for thy own strength and for thy own preparation--

Now I say unto thee my child - Thedra: This shall be read unto them at this time and they shall remember these my words and take heed of them - I say they shall heed them well.

And I am mindful of that which is said and done - and I go not out of my place that I might hear -- I am mindful of my oneness with God the Father - and I know myself to be - therefore I go not - neither do I come - I AM ---

And I say - when they have prepared themself I shall appear unto them and they shall see me and counsel with me. For this have they waited ---

I say I am not a fool and I am not easily deceived - I say that which is wise and prudent -- So be it I have spoken wisely and with love - and I am near unto thee and ye shall be blest of me and by me -- So be it and Selah ---

I am Sanat Kumara

Sister Thedra of the Emerald Cross

They are Not Alone - Not Self-Sufficient

While it is said that there shall be great action and steps shall be taken to awaken the sleeper - I say it is now come when many shall pass knowing not that the day of fulfillment is come - and these shall be given a place and a time - wherein to do that which they have not done.

That which hast not been finished this day shall be finished at another time, for there is a time of fulfillment, a time of sowing, a time of reaping and for them which wait, We say unto them: Wait no longer, for this is the day for which thou hast waited and for this do We now offer the assistance We are so able to give at this time.

While they know not that We are about and that We are their Benefactors, they hear not, neither do they see. They give unto Us no quarter, no credence, for they believe themself "self-sufficient" and alone. While We say thou art not alone! Thou art not self-sufficient!! Were We to forsake them they should perish, for it is by Our efforts that they are able to breathe, for by their effort have they polluted the ethers, the very air they breathe.

They have been so bold, so foolish as to blast the face of the earth with nefarious machinations. They have been so foolish as to blast the bowels of the Earth, the depth of the waters hast been at their mercy and they have desecrated the depth and the heights.

They know not that which they do, they set into motion the eth and it shall fall back upon them that which they put therein and the Earth shall give forth with one loud cry and She shall spew forth from Her bowels fire and water such as they have not seen. I say it shall be seen, and they shall cry out in horror and fear.

So I say unto them prepare thineself! For it is come when ye shall stand and cry Lord, Lord, Have mercy upon us.

I Am Sananda -

Recorded by Sister Thedra of the Emerald Cross

It is Not an Attempt to Subject a Nation or a People

Sori Sori - Beloved of Mine being - I speak unto thee of things concerning Spirit - things which are of great import. It is now time to say that the Ones which have been the Benefactors of the Earth and the family thereof shall be given assignments which shall pertain unto this "Action, which shall be taken"

The action of which We have spoken while it is of great import, it far exceeds thine imagination! It is not a puny attempt to subject a nation or a people.

It is an attempt to awaken them which are asleep on their feet. The ones in lethargy - This is the greater task! For they which are asleep know it not, they know not that they know not.

They dream the dreams of the sleepers and believe them to be real. They are the ones which I now address; I say unto them: Be ye as ones alert and hear ye that which I say unto thee - for ye shall be caught up short of thy course, for there is but a short while ere ye see that which shall be unto thee a great and mighty onrush of action which shall be strange and new unto thee.

Ye shall see and wonder, and ye shall be as ones afrightened, and ye shall run and hide and cry out for assistance.

I say <u>this is thine assistance</u> - fear not - be ye as ones prepared to accept it, for this are We prepared - We stand by to assist, yet ye shall be as ones prepared to accept Us and that which We offer, We say: "fear not!"

Look, See, and be glad for having seen. I say, ye shall ask for Light, and it shall be revealed unto thee, so be it. I am sent of Mine Father which hast given unto us being that ye be lifted up. Yet it is said many times ye shall first be of a mind to receive Us and of Us.

For We shall do Our part, yet the time draweth nigh when We shall be glad that We are within reach of thine call, for ye shall call! Call and We shall hear - We come that ye might be enlightened and prepared for such action as is now come. Be ye as one prepared to be lifted up.

While ye run hither and yon seeking signs and wonders and verification of thine opinions, ideas and wants and of the wants of the one which would set themselves up as authorities on Our activities I say unto thee I Am an Authority, for I have been at this for a long while, and I have seen the going and coming of them which are now bound unto the wheel of rebirth - So be it that We come that ye might be unbound - UNBOUND FOREVER! Never more to go into bondage.

So let it be as ye will it. I say: Let it be as ye will it - none shall be unto thee thine Savior - thine oppressor - ye come of thine own free will. None oppose it - for that is not our purpose. I am come that ye might have light. Let it be - I Am Sananda

Recorded by Sister Thedra of the Emerald Cross

They Pilfer Not the Secrets of the Inner Lodge

Sanat Kumara Speaking:

It is given unto Me to Know the Plan and for this do I say unto thee: be ye as Mine hand made manifest unto them and say unto them in Mine Name and as I would say unto them, that the way has been made clear before them, and they have been given the key into the Holy of Holies, yet I say it is given unto the traitors to look and not see - to look and not find for they have not been prepared that they see - they have not proven themself trustworthy, and none come into the inner temple as a thief in the night for We are watchful, and they pilfer not the secrets of the inner Lodge.

The Brothers of Light are not so foolish as to give unto them of their cup without their preparation. They cannot escape the law, and for that reason are We aware of Our actions of Our own part. We trespass not on that of another - neither do We give unto the unjust and the profane that which be unto them their undoing. It is given unto Us to be Custodians of the records the law is plainly written that thou shall not trespass upon thy brothers freewill.

That ye shall not give unto him the bitter cup - love thine Brother as thy own self, and wherein is it said that there is no more? Wherein do I find them which keepeth the law?

I say the law is exacting and none enter into the Holy of Holies unprepared - for this do I say be ye as ones prepared - apply the law unto thine ownself and be ye no part of their foolishness - look not yonder that ye might see their shortcomings, their misdeeds, look well unto thine own and be ye not dissuaded.

For therein is thine own shortcoming - ye shall be as ones alert, and ye shall cleanse out thine own closet and be ye not concerned with thine neighbors, while the moths consume thine own. Yet it behooves Me to warn thee of thine own shortcoming of thine own oversight, for thou art want to speak of thy brothers guilt and wherein art thou stainless? I bid thee look well into thine own secret places, and deceive not thine ownself - for therein is hypocrisy!

Look well into thine own closet and bring out that which thou has hidden therein and be ye wise and put it from thee with no guilt - for to turn from it and be no more part of it is to forgive thyself and it shall be unto thee thine freedom. Follow ye the example which our Brother Sananda hast given thee.

Let it be said to forgive thine ownself is to be no part of that which hast been done and said which hast given pain and misery unto another and worse unto thine own self, for all that which thou hast directed unto thine fellow man in hatred, malice or in anger hast the way of returning unto thee to torment thee.

Turn from thine own way and be ye as one enlightened. Be ye filled with love for thine brothers, be he of the specie of man or animal -- for this is thine time of forgiveness - forgive thyself and ye shall repeat it no more. Let it suffice that I am come to bring peace unto the troubled hearts. I am Sanat Kumara

Recorded by Sister Thedra of the Emerald Cross

Self Service
(Do it yourself)

Blest art they which come unto this altar for they art blest of Me and by Me - for they art with Me and they shall be blest when it is come that they shall choose which way they shall go, they shall choose Mine way for nothing else matters.

I say unto thee: Ye have now chosen Me, Mine Way - let nothing turn thee aside, for this do I place Mine Hand upon thee and give unto thee these words - Let it be unto thee thine shield and thine buckler in the time of stress - too, I say unto thee the days of stress is not past - for it is given unto Me to see the way before thee, and there shall be times of stress, yet this shall be thine time of testing.

The time of testing is not done - and for this do I say put on the whole armor of God. Gird up thine self and bless thine own self in the going - for none other shall be thine carter - it is a "Self Service" and none shall be unto thee the doer, it is thine own armor that ye shall wear for none other shall be available unto thee. Be ye blest this day for I am come that ye be blest - I Am Sananda

Recorded by Sister Thedra of the Emerald Cross

They Shall Be Known as the Trail Blazers

Beloved ones: While I am thy Sibor, thine Older Brother, I am prepared to give unto thee this word, and it is for the good of all, so let them partake of this portion which I now give unto thee - for this do I give it unto thee - that ye might record it for them.

While it is not given unto all to hear that which I say, it is given unto thee to have ears which hear that which I say, it is indeed a great gift - for which thou hast prepared thyself.

Now let it be given unto them thusly: the time is come when the ones which have come into the world of flesh for the purpose of mentoring or being unto thee the ears, the eyes, the feet - the parts which function from the Higher Level - these shall become known unto thee as the "Trail Blazers" - they have gone before thee knowing that theirs was a part which brought no reward from man - yet for the greater part only suffering and persecution - while the unknowing ones thought themself wise, they jeered and taunted, and for that matter made foolish saying unto and about them, these "Trail-Blazers". Yet it is now come when ye shall come to know, that they knew of which they spoke - yet I say ye shall be mindful of them, and of thine own foolishness, for it shall rebound back to confront thee and ye shall be as ones affronted with thine foolish sayings for they shall come before thee to taunt thee.

Let thine lips be swift - to retract them and make restitution unto them which thou hast persecuted, be ye swift to ask of them forgiveness, lend a hand when possible to assist in this the day of learning - the day of enlightenment. Be ye swift to assist in the deliverance from bondage and darkness. I say ye shall first be enlightened, <u>then</u> ye shall know; it is said, first seek ye the light and it shall not be denied thee.

Now it shall be said that the "Trail-Blazers" have gone before thee as the "Spearmen" that thy way be made clear before and these are the ones strong of character and filled with the water of Spirit - the water that quenches the thirst of them which doth hunger for Light, truth and justice. I say these are Mine "Spearmen", Mine "Plowmen", they have gone before Me to make fertile the soil for the seed of the new day which now dawns in the East, I say it dawns in the East - be ye up and about the work of the "New Day". Sleep not while it is dawning, for all nature cries out. Awaken! Awaken! Look, See!

Behold! and rejoice - for the new day breaks forth with a glad shout, Arise! Come ye forth from out the pit - Let thine heart be swift to rejoice!

For I am come that ye Awaken! Be ye blest this day, I am Sanat Kumara

Recorded by Sister Thedra of the Emerald Cross

The Fulfillment of All the Promises

Beloved Ones - Unto thee I say behold this day the hand of God move. Look, See, and Know ye that it moves in ways ye know not, for this is it said, be ye as ones prepared - for to be prepared ye shall know - to know is to be prepared - to know is wisdom.

For this I am come, that ye might know - this day I would say unto thee, be ye as ones prepared to receive Me and of Me - to know me, to receive me is the better part of thine preparation, for when thou hast prepared thineself to receive Me and of Me, then I shall come unto thee and I shall give unto thee the part which I have kept for thee, and this part shall be the part which shall be the fulfillment of all the promises, on the covenant, which we have made long since, which hast not been made invalid by time, space or thine unknowing.

I say it is valid, and it is Mine Word unto thee and I shall not be unto thee a traitor neither unto Mineself or Mine trust, the illusion of time hast been unto thee a great veil through which thou seest but faintly, thou hast wearied of thine waiting and fallen asleep - and for this do I say: "Awaken all ye which sleepeth".

So let it be for I shall call again and again, I have sent Mine plowmen, Mine spearmen out before Me and the soil shall be made ready and I shall enter into to the world of men as one of them and I shall find them by the Light which they are, by their own light shall they be found, therefore I say keep thine own lamp oiled and burning, let thine Light so shine that others might see it and be drawn unto it.

For this it is said: Let there be Light - Let there be Light within thee! And ye shall not be overlooked. Be ye as ones prepared to receive Me, the Mighty Host, and We shall not forsake thee in the time of stress, So be it and Selah - I am Sananda

THE ACTION WHICH IS NOW BEING TAKEN

By what hand shall they be spared? By what hand shall they be brought out?

By What Power?

By What Authority?"

I ask of them by what hand hast thou been sustained? By Whose grace hast thou been spared - By Whose Wisdom?

Now let it be said:

Were it not for the wisdom which is endowed unto Us of the Father, thou wouldst not endure - thou wouldst not be able to breathe for it is by the consolidated efforts of the great and mighty Host and the Grand Council that the action hast been taken which shall become apparent unto thee: Unto the dense ones - unto them which yet sleepeth!

I say the action which is now being taken shall become apparent unto each and every one which has one iota of comprehension.

I too say that We are not so foolish as to fall asleep - for there is much to be done - Let it be said that at no time in man's history hast he been able to bear witness of such action as is now taking place within the realms of Light and within the realms of the seen, for the action of which I speak shall be seen and felt within the world of man, yet I say they have not seen such as they shall see - for it shall be unlike any other action which has hitherto been enacted upon the Earth! I say man hast not witnessed that which he shall witness for he hast not been aware of that which hast first taken place on the planes just above that of the material world - the place in which he now functions, and that which he is aware of - for this do We say - "Be ye aware of that which goes on about thee and many things shall be revealed unto thee, so be it, I speak out for the sake of all which have a mind to hear me. So let them hear, for none other shall hear.

I am with thee that they be alerted. So be it.

I am Sananda

Recorded by Sister Thedra of the Emerald Cross

They See as Through Lenses Born of Conflict

Beloved Ones: This is Mine time and I shall give unto thee this word for them which doth aspire unto the heights. Let them aspire - let them attain - let them be as the ones to attain.

And give unto them credit for their own attainment. Let it be remembered they are not alone - for we the "Host" are here that we might assist them in their attainment.

Let it be said that they see as through lenses born of conflict - they see not clearly, for were it not for the "Mighty Host" they should never know - they should never see - for they have been so long in darkness they have been blinded by the light.

Now it is released a portion at a time as they can bear it. As they are conditioned unto it, and it is not our purpose to blind them, neither give them more than they can consume - so be it that We work with the Plan which shall be revealed in due season (unto them which prove themself trustworthy.)

Let it be understood that each portion goes forth with a blessing and a touch which shall profit them. I say these portions are not to be overlooked for each is part of the whole and not one word is to be discounted or overlooked, they are designed for a purpose, for the Candidate - the Aspirant, and at no time is he to lay aside the portions as of no import.

I say they are so designed to benefit the aspirant - the Candidate for the Great Initiation - the "Greater part".

Be ye as ones which know and give unto thine brother a hand yet give him not of thine cup which hast not prepared himself. He shall first make ready himself, then he shall drink and be satisfied - let him not ride thine back - let him put forth his own effort and energy that he might earn the right to drink of thine cup and to call himself a Sibet or Brother. The word Brother is not to be taken lightly within this Order. First they prove themself, they shall earn the right to be called Brother. It is a privilege ye know?

Wherefore hast thou found thy way? Hast thou found it the easy way? Yet thou hast found great joy in serving me - in thine selfless service. Let them too learn as thou hast learned. Let them too share the joy, and be blest. Let not thine heart be troubled for them.

Yet ye shall place before them these "portions" that they might be prepared for the greater part. Yet ye shall not trespass upon their free will. Do not push thine own part upon them for it is the foolishness of babes - the better part of wisdom is the example which thou shall set before them.

Let not thine lips belie thine heart - deceive not thine own self. And let thine own feet be swift to do Mine work. Thine hands swift to do that which I shall give unto thee to do. Let thine tongue be swift to declare the glory of the Lord - to bear witness of Me that I am come. Yet ye shall first be prepared to receive Me and of Me then I shall reveal Mineself unto thee.

I am Sananda

Recorded by Sister Thedra of the Emerald Cross

I am Come Declaring the Truth

Be ye as Mine hand made manifest unto them, and say unto them in Mine Name that there is but one Lord God - and it is not robbery to declare it - for it is given unto Me to say so - for Mine Father hast sent Me forth in His Name and by His grace I come declaring the Truth that they might know that I am come.

Yet it is said many shall come in Mine Name - while it is clearly stated that there shall be whisperings and murmurings, I say that I am He which is sent that there be Light, and they which deny Me also deny Mine Father which hast sent Me forth, for the Father and I are one.

Now for the ones which look for gods in strange places - and seek out the 'wise' and gifted of tongue - I say unto them be ye aware for I am not of a mind to impersonate them - I am not come to give unto thee signs and wonders, therein is foolishness! I am come that ye be lifted up - that ye might have Light - I am the Way and the Light, and I am come that ye might know - for to Know is Wisdom.

It is said that there are none so foolish as the one which thinks himself wise! So be it - he is one which betrays himself, as one which throws overboard his own lifebelt. So be it the pity of the foolish - they babble as ones which know not the true from the false.

I Am one which knows - So be it - I am Sananda, Son of God.

I Come as a Thief in the Night

Be ye as Mine Hand made manifest and say unto them in Mine Name and as I would that when they have put from them all hatred, all uncleanliness, untruth, deceit, dishonor, and discord, I shall come unto them and I shall counsel them and I shall make Mine self known unto them. Then they shall know Me for a surety.

This day I say unto them: be ye as one prepared to receive Me and of Me. Yet wherein do I find them prepared??

Let them first prepare themself to receive Me - and then I shall come unto THEM!

Wherein is it said this is the day of preparation? Yet they wait! Let their hearts be softened, their tongues be silenced, their hands be cleansed, that I might use them, that I might come into their midst and be one with them.

I say, I go not into the den of the porcupines - I go not into the dragon's den - for it is said that there is not room for the two to occupy at the same time.

I say: They serve Me with both hands. I do not accept one while the other serves the dragon - they shall devote themself wholeheartedly unto Me for I am sent that they be brought out of bondage - So let them apply themself untiring - Unconditionally unto the task at hand, <u>that of their own freedom</u>!

So let it be as they will it, I but stand by to assist - I say I stand by for a time, yet time runs out - and then they shall know the folly of their waiting. So be it that I come - I go - No man knew the hour of Mine coming. As the thief in the night I came - as the thief in the night I shall go - for I shall not announce the time of Mine going when I shall go as with a great and mighty onrush of water with the Great and Mighty Host which shall accompany Me - for it is said that the Host awaits Mine departure, and then the ones so prepared shall go even as I go - they shall arise as on wings - and they shall return unto the Father with Me.

Let it be understood - that none shall be brought against their own will - for We come not to transgress the law - rather that it be fulfilled. So be it, We Know that which We are about so let it be revealed unto them which have the will to follow Me, for where I go they too shall go - but to deny Mine Word is to deny Me - to deny Me is to deny Mine Father which hast sent Me. So be it, I come that they might be lifted up. So be it that I am the Lord thy God - Sananda

Recorded by Sister Thedra of the Emerald Cross

To the Ones in High Places

Sanat Kumara speaking -

Ye shall now give unto them this word and it shall go out unto all which are of a mind to learn -

I say unto them that it is now come when they shall be as ones which have burned the midnite oil and they have wasted their substance for they have sown unto the wind - They have been as the ones which have gathered unto themself tares and thistles - I say they have wasted their substance - and they have not taken thought of the Father which has given unto them being - Now I say unto them they have given unto themself credit for being wise when they have been the greatest of fools. I say they have been fools -

Now I say unto them which sit in high places that there are none so foolish as the one which thinks himself wise and none so sad as he which betrays himself or his trust - for it is now come when the traitors shall be brought to account for his foolishness - and he shall be as one cast out - I say he shall be as one cast out - For he has not reckoned with the law. He has not given credit where credit is due - He has not been unto himself true.

Nor has he been unto his trust true. He has been unto himself traitor, he has bartered in human sacrifice, he has been as one which has upon his hand the blood of the saints - the blood of his children and the blood of his brother. I say he has even sacrificed his father and mother that he be given the privilege of serving the one cast down - the dragon. I say he shall come to know that which has held him bound hand and foot to be the dragon - which has gone the long way to bind him -

Now I say unto thee which have a mind to learn that there are none so sad as the one which betrays his trust - for he shall suffer the consequences - and he shall be as one cast out.

For the first time I say unto them which betray themself that they shall go unto a place which is prepared for them wherein they shall begin at the beginning - They shall have their memory blanked from them and they shall know not that which they now boast of - the knowledge of which they boast shall be as naught. And all their opinions shall go as the chaff before the wind.

I speak unto them which are so minded to serve the forces of darkness - and when ye have given of thyself that ye may be glorified and thy appetites satisfied, ye shall be as ones which have given of thy strength and of thyself that thy brother may suffer that which is unbearable. And I say woe unto any man which gives unto his brother the bitter cup. Such is my word unto thee and ye shall study well these my words - for ye shall have cause to remember them.

I am come that they may be delivered up which have a mind unto peace and them which have a mind unto learning I shall give unto them wisdom and peace which no man shall take from them and I am of the mind to give unto them as I have received of the Father - Such is my inheritance that I am one with the Father and all the Father has is mine to give - for He has endowed unto me all that He is and all that He has. And for this do I say - be ye as one prepared for to receive me and of me - for inasmuch as ye do receive me ye shall receive the Father and as ye receive Him and of Him - So shall ye receive thy Godhood - Amen and Selah - I am thy older brother - Sanat Kumara

Recorded by Sister Thedra

I Did Say: I Shall Return

Behold - I Am Come! - The One which hast awaited this day when I might walk among them which hast kept their covenant with Me -- I say unto <u>them</u>: I Am come that Mine Part might be fulfilled -- I say unto them - I come that ye might go where I go ---

Now! It is come when I have returned unto thee for the purpose of fulfilling Mine Promise - Mine Covenant - that it might be finished THIS DAY -- Never wast it finished - for I did say: "I shall return unto thee that where I go ye might go also" -- So let it be ---

For this - do I say unto thee - be ye about thine preparation that it might be so -- So let it be as the <u>Father</u> <u>hast</u> <u>Willed</u> <u>it</u> - I come that His Will be done in Me - through Me - and by Me - <u>this</u> <u>day</u> -- So let it be. I say unto thee - let it be done! For I Am come unto thee that it be done as He hast sent Me for that purpose -- Call unto them which hast ears to hear - and say unto them as I would say - that "He is come that where He goes ye might go also" -- So let them hear that which I say <u>this</u> <u>day</u>. Be it the Truth and the Light by which they shall come ---

I give unto thee of Mineself that they might come to know Me -- So be it they that have <u>ears</u> <u>to</u> <u>hear</u> - shall know Mine Voice and respond unto it ---

Let thine Light so shine that they MIGHT FOLLOW IT.

So be it I Am the Lord thy God

Sananda

Recorded by Sister Thedra of the Emerald Cross

The Fulfilling of the Scriptures the Law

Sanat Kumara Speaking -- Mine Beloved Ones - It is said of this day - it shall be the Greatest the Earth hast known for it shall be the fulfilling of All the Promises - for that matter it is the Fulfillment of the "Scriptures", the Fulfilling of the Law.

While it is said there is a time and a place - and a part - there is a time for the fulfilling and a time for the promises- Yet I say they have waited for the Fulfillment and the time is now come when the Law shall be fulfilled - And then it shall be given unto Us of the Great and Grand Council to come forth and Set Up such a Government as thou hast not known.

Yet it is said that that which wast given unto thee in the beginning, at the Founding of thy Great Nation wast so dictated and set forth by and of This Body -- Yet it hast not been unto the fulfillment for man hast altered the Concept of the Founding fathers -- They have not been true unto the precepts of the Great and Mighty "Word" which was given unto them for the purpose of setting up such a Government as might function within this Body - and serve the children of Earth as We serve as the Selfless Body which is the Greater Part of Service --

We now sit in Council that others be raised up for the purpose of Serving the Plan - and for this are They taking upon Themself flesh bodies: vehicles of flesh that They might Serve in the material world as men - as the Servants of this Mighty Council - And it is given unto them to be Prepared for Their Part ere They come into flesh - Yet they shall Grow into Maturity as other children of Earth - yet when the time comes that They take Their place within the Affairs of Government We shall be unto Them all that they shall need - for We shall remember Them and know Them as Our Own --

I say: "We forsake Not Our Own" - Theirs is a Mission of Sacrifice. They come of Their own Will - yet for that matter They have no Will other than to Serve that the Earth and Her Children be lifted up --

Now ye shall not speculate on These which come for I say it shall be known Only unto Us - for it is a well Guarded Secret - We Know the value of Silence - We too Know the wanton ones - the traitors. So be it they shall be of no moment unto the Plan - for We have the Plan and We Know that which shall be done - and none shall deter Us from Our Goal which is to Set Up a Kingdom upon the Earth under the Banner of the Cross and the Crown

And We say Hail unto the Victors!!

Let it be understood that there shall be Many to Assist in this Plan.

Let it be as ye Will it -

I AM

The Grand Master

Within the Inner Temple --

I AM Sanat Kumara

Recorded by Sister Thedra of the Emerald Cross

We of the Mighty Host Hast Revealed Our Presence

Behold, this day the Glory of the Lord! Behold this day the Mighty Work which shall be done!

For it is Now Come when the Mighty Host shall Come Closer unto the Earth and Greater shall be the Light -- And Great Knowledge shall be the fortune of them which have the Mind and the Will to learn --

For this have We of the Mighty Host revealed Our Presence and it shall become More Apparent unto them which have eyes to see -

Let All the Nations Stand Still - Look and See - Let All the Nations lay aside their Weapons and be unto each other Brothers --

For they shall see the folly of their Own Way - Their own Foolishness shall be unto them the Torment which shall plague them - it shall not be Ours - neither of Our doing! I say Neither of Our Doing!

Let them learn well the lesson of Brotherly Love -- Then they shall know that Brotherly Love prompts Our Action -- And then they shall be as ones Prepared to join with us in the Great Plan for the Freedom of All Men Everywhere -- So let it be as they are prepared --

Now let it be said that We - of the Host shall do that which We have been given to do and neither time - tide nor man shall Stay Us - for the time is Now Come when Certain Action shall be taken and they shall be Caused to lay down their weapons, and they shall take them up no more - for they shall know the foolishness of conflict one with the other.

This is not the easiest way - the lesser task for Us - Yet it is the Greater - The Greater Task is to Teach Man Love One for the Other -

Yet to see him slay his brother - then to set up monuments unto him is the fortune of the one which has his head bound by the black hood -he sees not - he knows not the Love which prompts Our actions -- for Our Acts are Acts of Mercy - and Wisdom and designed to bring them out of bondage --

They have misinterpreted Our Presence - Our Actions - Our Word, The Words given unto them for the purpose of bringing them OUT OF BONDAGE - yet they have slaughtered the Messengers - their Avatars they have martyred - slain and ridiculed -- Then set up Shrines - Altars to them and prayed unto them Asking Alms!!

I say they Know Not the Abhorrence of such a State of being -- they are Bound by the Dragon!!

Now We shall step in and make Ourself Known - Our Presence shall be felt in All the Nations of the Earth - and the Peoples thereof shall lift up their eyes and see that We are Not talking unto Ourself for the sheer joy of hearing Ourself speak - We have no need for words. We Know! We are not confused! Their words which escape their lips are seen for what they Are -- they Are Seen for that which they Are - they confuse Us NOT!!!

They but betray themself by their deeds -- they speak of LOVE -- PEACE -- And it is not within them, it is NOT established Within THEM ------

Let it be established within their hearts - THEN they shall Know as the Great and Mighty Ones shall Enlighten them --

Let it be!

For THIS have We spoken out --

I AM the LORD of HOSTS

I AM that I AM

Preparation & Loyalty

Beloved Ones -- This day let it be said that None Other is responsible for thee - Thine preparation - While it is said that there are many which stand by to give Assistance - it is given unto thee to prepare thy own self for to receive it for They give as thou art prepared to receive - So let it profit thee - for They are not wont to give unto thee that which would torment thee - It is given unto Them to be thy Benefactors for without Them ye should be a pitiful lot! So be it that it is Now Come when ye shall stand Firm - Steadfast - upon the Rock which I AM –

So be it that I have spoken. Much of Preparation - and Loyalty is not the lessor part - for to be trustworthy is one of the requirements of Character - wherein the Great "White Brotherhood" is concerned - So be it that I speak for the whole of the Brotherhood and I Know that which I Say - So be it that I AM the Lord thy God --

Sananda

Recorded by Sister Thedra of the Emerald Cross

The Reaping

Blessed are they which walk with me,

Blessed are they which know Me,

Blessed are they which counsel with Me --

For they shall be as Ones prepared to enter into the Place wherein I AM - For this have I said Come - follow ye Me --

For this have I given unto thee - The Laws that ye might apply them that ye be prepared--

For this have I given of Mineself that ye be prepared - Let it be so.

Now let it be understood that Ours is a Mission of Selfless Service.

For We of the Host have a Choice wherein We might Serve - Yet We Know the Great Need of the Moment - which is This One which We have responded unto At This Moment.

Let it be said now that there are Ones which walk in the flesh which have come as the ones which have the Same Calling - that of Selfless Service --

While They Ask Nought save the privilege of Serving in the Plan I say They too have born the Cross - for man has betrayed himself by his own deeds - acts - words - and thoughts - for they have given unto the Messengers the Emissaries and their Prophets the Bitter Cup! -- They have added unto their suffering and torment --

I say the ones which have been Their persecutors shall this day be as ones bowed down with sorrow - for they shall come to know that which they have given out - They too shall receive in FULL MEASURE and not one shall escape - for this is the day of Fulfillment,- the day of Balancing thine Account - let it be Balanced --

So be it, it shall profit thee.

I am Come that ye might Know these things thereby be prepared for such as shall be given unto thee for as ye are prepared - So shall ye receive -- Let it bring Joy and Peace unto thee --

I AM Sananda

Recorded by Sister Thedra of the Emerald Cross

Concerning the Higher & Lower Councils of Government

Blessed Ones: Let this be said for the good of all mankind, let it be recorded that they might know that which goes on about them - I say there are Ones which now sit in "High"* Places which are prepared to step forth and do a Mighty Work - and it shall be for the good of all, and unto the glory of the Father for I say that These of which I speak sit in the High Places prepared to come forth at the appointed hour and do that which is given unto Them to do.

They have been prepared for Their part and They know what it is that They are to do. While They have had to wait certain Signs, and Word, They have been prepared as none others, for long have They waited.

When it is said that These have been prepared that They might glorify the Father - honor Him, I too say, that there are ones which also sit in places of "high honor"** which have betrayed their trust. These shall be as ones dishonored and disregarded, these shall be put out in dishonor and in disregard of their high place or seat in government and they shall be as ones exposed.

They shall be as ones which shall be justly accused and none shall be unto them the "Savior" for they shall account for their dishonor and unfaithfulness unto their office and trust.

I say that the time is come when they shall no longer hide behind a cloak of respectability - they shall be exposed - So let it be. I am come that there be light and that justice be done in all things. So let it be.

I am the Lord thy God - Sananda

Recorded by Sister Thedra of the Emerald Cross

*The illumined of God - of the "Great and Mighty Council"

** Earth government/ Worldly government.

The One to Come
Forewarning

Were it not for the Host this Communication Would Not be possible - for it is by the Consolidated Efforts that We of the Host have Made it possible --

Now let this be understood - the Written Word is the lesser of the Revelation - for it is of necessity that the Written Word be brief - yet the Word which goes forth Unwritten - Unrecorded on Paper - Parchment - Stone - shall be Heard and Remembered as if Written upon the Most Imperishable Substance!

I say It Shall Be Remembered!

And No man shall pilfer it - when it is Written Upon Thine Heart - for then it is Thine to Have and to Hold - Thine to Keep, and to Know this is the Imperishable Word - which shall pass Not Away - I say it shall not pass Away - At No Time shall it be taken away from thee - for it shall be Deeply Imprinted Within Thine Own Being - and Become Part of thine Own Record --

I speak unto them which have ears to hear - let them hear. They which Hear shall know that which I say - the ones which reads the "letter" shall not hear for they but concern themself with the letter - they see not that which lies Hidden between - I say Look Again - See that which is Hidden within the Recorded Word for it shall be unto thee the cover which hides the "Priceless Pearl" which ye shall seek to find --

Let it be found and Treasured - So be it that I have taken care to Cover Mine Precious Gems with the letter --

I say Discount Not the covering - for it too is of Great Value - hast it not been given unto thee from thy Benefactors which have Guarded Thee So Diligently and Lovingly?

I say They have Planned Well Their Word - Chosen Well Their Words - that ye be not burdened with Great and Profuse wording - which but Astound and Bewilder thee. We come that All might share in Our Fortune - for this has the Father Sent Us -- So be it I ask of thee Be Considerate of Thine Own Welfare and give Credit where Credit is due - let Not thine hands betray thine heart - let Not thine Tongue betray thee - be ye as one which can See the "Hand-writing on the Wall" and the Meaning Thereof shall be interpreted - or Revealed unto <u>thee</u> - I say Ye shall KEEP THINE OWN COUNSEL - Ask of No Man his opinion, his counsel - on the Word - or thine way to go - for I say <u>he</u> <u>too</u> walks in flesh - Yet I have said that "One shall be Sent" I have said "Ask and ye shall receive" Yet ask not of man - ask of the Father which hast Sent Me -- and He shall send One unto thee which Knows thine every Need,- thine EVERY need - and there shall be no need for words - Question Not the One which is Sent - for He shall bear His Own Authority With Dignity and Honor.

He shall be humble of heart - He shall walk becomingly at All times there shall be no boastfulness - no hypocrisy within him - He shall be unto thee Great Light - and He shall bless thee by His Presence - let Him be known herein as the Brother Which has come for thy sake - So be it that He is sent of Me - I bear Witness of Him - So be it that I forewarn thee of His coming--

I AM Sananda

Recorded by Sister Thedra of the Emerald Cross

The Great & Mighty Host is Come Closer

Beloved Ones: It is now time to give unto thee this part - And it shall be given in parts - So be it the better part of Wisdom.

It is Mine Part to give unto thee this Word - And it is so designed and sent forth as to awaken them which sleepeth - I say these which yet sleepeth shall be awakened - While there are ones which have not the will to awaken - these shall sleep on - While I say they shall sleep on - they too shall awaken in a new place - and a new day - Yet they shall wait long - for it is the day of Awakening NOW!

While I say This IS the day of Awakening - I too say that there shall be another - and it shall be long ere it comes -- So let it be said: them that wait shall find it long and hard --

Wherein is it said that their sleep shall be long and troubled!

It now comes when the Great and Mighty Host IS Come Closer unto the Earth - That All might be blest of Their Presence - <u>by</u> Their Presence - And it is given unto Me to be One of the Host - therefore I Am qualified to Speak out - It is for this that I Am permitted this Joy of Serving in this capacity - that of Sibor unto thee -- I speak unto All which are of a mind to accept US - and that which we bring unto thee.

It is given unto Us to be a Great Number and of Great Power - For the Father hast invested within Us the Power and the Authority to bring Us a Plan so designed to bring them out of bondage - darkness - They shall be as ones prepared to Receive Us - and of Us - for WE are Not Allowed by law to give unto them that which shall bring about any torment unto them - Yet I say they shall be as ones shocked to learn of Our Existence - Our Nature - and Our MISSION - for it has been carefully concealed from them - they have not imaged that which they shall Come to Know for a Surety - Yet it is Now time that they be Alerted and Awakened -- It is given unto Me to see them slowly arousing themself from Sheer Necessity - for it behooves them to pick up their feet and Get in Step with the Ones which Know - and which are of the Great White Brotherhood - for These are the ones Illumined These are the Ones which Work Unceasingly - without thought of reward for Their Benefit - for Their Enlightenment -- The ones which have thought themself wise shall See that which they have Not seen - they shall Know they have Not Known! That they have <u>not</u> been Wise!

So be it that I shall Speak unto them At Great Length that it be So.

So let it be --

Recorded by Sister Thedra of the Emerald Cross

We Come Solely Because of Our Love

Beloved Ones:

The offer of Sight is the Promise given - And it is thine when thou art Prepared to Receive it -- I say unto thee thine eyes could Not Endure the Glory of God - Thine eyes Could Not Behold It - So Great is His Glory -- I speak unto thee of Light which thou Knowest Not Of - For Such Light thou hast Not Seen --

Let it be said that there is None which could endure the Grandeur of His Presence - for this does it become necessary to dim thine eyes that ye see but faintly - as through A Veil Darkly - yet the veil shall be removed in time - And So Great shall be thy Joy that ye shall be as ones Transfixed - And thine Being shall be filled with Joy - and then ye shall turn to give unto thine faltering brothers a hand even as We thine older Brothers have given of Ours that ye be lifted up --

So be it that WE Come Solely because of Our Love and Compassion for thee -- Thine unknowing is a pitiful plight and for this hast it been of Our Own Will that We offer Our Assistance - that ye too might come to Know such Joy - Let it be - For We of the Mighty Host shall be as the Host -- We shall be as the Ones which shall Sing out with Great Joy When thou hast been liberated from bondage --

And for this do WE Wait --

Be ye blest of Me and by Me

for I Am Come that ye be blest

So let it be --

I AM Sananda

Recorded by Sister Thedra of the Emerald Cross

The Emissaries from the Great Assembly

Beloved Ones: This day let it be known unto thee that the Way is now prepared before thee that ye might make thine own way into the Place wherein I am. I say it is with Tireless Effort that We of the "Great and Mighty Assembly" have worked for this day. Not one which has Their Part with the Assembly is unmindful of thee.

Not one is overlooked, for the Assembly Comprises the Ones which have gone the "Royal Road" - and they have NOT lost THEIR Memory as thou hast. It is for this that they have Great Compassion on, and for, thee. When it is given unto the flesh to tire They Know that which is indeed the Weakness of flesh - They Know that which is Strength of Spirit - and it is Their Part to replenish the Strength and Energy when and where necessary --

Yet let this be said: none shall put the responsibility of their weakness upon the Ones which have so lovingly assisted in the hours of their unknowing and weakness. Ask of Them naught save Their Assistance. They know that which is necessary. It is for thy own Willingness to Receive Them and be One with Them that enables Them to assist thee, for it is not the time neither the place to come unto thee in the form of flesh.

While it is said that They do walk with thee in flesh, They do not reveal themself for the entertainment thereof. They do not flaunt Themself, They walk in Silence and They are Not given unto boasting. They Know where They go, what They do and They are about the Father's Business even as ye and I.

For They have a Mission and it shall be terminated in a Great and Glorious Success - and not one shall be as the Advisor unto those which are the "Emissaries" from this Great Assembly - I say They are Well Trained - and Self Sufficient - They are as the "Trail blazers" They are the "Spear men" They are as the "Plowmen" gone forth to prepare the Way for the Great and Glorious Day when the Host of Hosts shall Come forth in a Great Blaze of Glory - and then Their Mission shall be finished and They shall no more be given the part to work with man --

For in that day man of Earth shall be lifted up - and no longer shall it be necessary to send forth the Ambassadors - the Messengers of the Mighty Council - for they shall not be bound in darkness neither shall the ones left have the Communication which is Now fortuned unto them for the ones left shall be left without Comfort- and they shall cry out for assistance. Yet We say late! Thou art late! We have departed and thou hast Not given unto Us Credit for Knowing that which We have said unto thee - Now ye shall wait in darkness - It behooves each and every one to alert themself and put aside their Willful Ways and prepare for the GREATER PART for I say unto them: None are brought into the Place wherein We Abide unprepared - for We are under the Law - the "Galactic Law" which forbids it --

We Know the Law, therefore Abide by it for We have not the mind of the Traitor - We give of Ourself that All be prepared - yet We have A Responsibility unto the WHOLE and not the few. So be it I am Not responsible for their Wilfullness and Wonton -- I come bringing with Me a Mighty Host and I make Mine Self Known unto the Ones So Prepared to Receive Me --

And unto these I reveal Mine Precepts and I Speak for the Whole of the Council - for I am the Head of this Council and I am Prepared to Speak -- When they have put aside their preconceived ideas, NOTIONS of Me and About Me and devoted themself wholeheartedly unto Mine Work, given of themself selflessly, then I shall reveal Mineself and they shall Know Me.

So be it I have spoken and thou hast heard - Give these Mine Words unto the Ones which have a mind to receive of Me and which are of a mind to follow Me - then I shall lead them -- Let them Choose which way --

Let it be as they Will it --

So be it I AM the Lord thy God

Known herein as Sananda

Son of God --

Without Understanding There is No Communication

Beloved Ones: With these Words I shall bless thee for they are so designed that ye be blest - When there is communication One with the Other there is Understanding and Without Understanding there is NO Communication -- And there is no communication when one cuts himself off one from the other - for this is it said be ye as "One" let there be understanding - And Communication --

While I say Words are the lesser part of communication and therein is the pity of it for there is too much reliance put upon the spoken word which but gives the smallest significance unto the Truth - for the Reality is Never conveyed by Words - or Language - such as thou art accustomed to -- While the Greater Revelation is Conveyed by way of Light Sources which they know so little of - and which shall be as the future means of communication –

These Light Rays shall Carry Great Power - Great Weight and Nothing shall bar or distort these Rays - for they shall be directed unto the ones prepared to receive - and at no time shall they be intercepted by the enemy which would destroy and distort and use them to their own end or nefarious schemes - I say they shall not pilfer such Power - neither shall they distort the Light for their own end --

So let it be said that WE are Masters of such Light Rays - Beams - and We Know the Law governing such as and therein is Another Story.- Be ye as Ones Prepared to receive it--

For it shall be given unto thee --

I AM thy Sibor and thy Older Brother

Berean

Recorded by Sister Thedra of the Emerald Cross

The Plan is Given in Parts

Beloved Ones: This day let it be recorded that which shall be given unto them which have a mind to receive it -- While I say there are ones which are not of a mind to accept those Mine Words - it is for the Ones which will to know the Truth. While there are Ones which have one part of the Whole, others have another part, yet none shall deny that which is given unto the other for the Great Plan shall be revealed only in part - until one is FULLY liberated from all bondage -- then he shall see and Know the Fullness of the Plan --

Now I say unto thee deny not that which another hast been Given for therein is folly - It is said that when they So Love Each Other that they put their Parts together On The Council Table they shall come to See the Whole of the Plan -- Let them Become Wise! Let them so Love each other that they put all their efforts into the gaining of Light - The Ones which are of the Great and Mighty Council shall then give unto them Greater Revelation - and they shall walk humbly and upright before the Great Tribunal And they shall be as ones Prepared to partake of such Knowledge as is Available through the Council -

While it is said they shall first be found trustworthy, We ask of thee Are they which strut themself and think themself prepared to drink of our Cup? I say unto thee, they shall first learn to Love One Another - They shall not revile against one another - they shall put from them All bigotry - All foolishness - idolatry - All puny ways -- they shall ask no penny for their service which shall be rendered in Love and in the Name of the Father, they shall set up no monuments unto their own imagery they shall at All times be as the Keepers of the Law -- They shall find no hiding place - for there is no hiding place. They shall Give of themself in humility and Love - for LOVE is not puffed up - it flaunts not itself, it is that which prompts Selfless Service --

Let this be Mine Word unto them which are of a mind to Know the fullness of the Plan - So be it I Am the "Host of Hosts" I Am He - which is Sent that the Way be prepared before thee - I say Prepare thineself for to receive the fullness of the Mighty Plan - And therein shall be the beginning and the end of thine learning - for it hast its beginning and end within the Realms of Light wherein there is No darkness - no limitation and no man enters into the Holy of Holies save by Me for I Am the Truth the Light and the Way - I Am the Door through which he enters -

I Say Behold Me the Door -

I Am - He Which Cometh Unto Thee that ye might be brought into the Place wherein there is no darkness wherein there is no limitation, wherein All is Known. So let it be that I Am the One Sent of Mine Father that it be so - So let it be -

Sananda

Recorded by Sister Thedra of the Emerald Cross

The Sacred Rites of Procreation

Be ye as Mine Hand made manifest unto them and say unto them as I would that there is but One Father over All - ALL - IN ALL - Not one has the part of the Father Save HIM - the Eternal Parent - Solen Aum Solen -- the One which hast given unto Us Being - For of Himself has He made Us His Children - He hast given of His Being that We might express HIM - that We might Glorify Him -- He hast given of Himself that We His Sons might have Individuality - He hast given unto Us Free Will and set Us apart over all other Creatures which fly - creep - or crawl upon the Land - in the seas or in the air --

Yet He hast made Us custodians of the lesser Creatures that they too might have their form of expression - that they might fulfill their part and become that for which they were given Being - each unto his own species. Never shall they become Adulterated as before - For this is it said that thou shalt Not Commit Adultery - It is given unto Man to be Sensuous in his desires and he knows No Limits for he has been as Ones Blinded unto the Results of his sensuousness - and he has not taken thought of the Law which shall hold him Accountable for his Misused Energy - I say he is bound by the Law - under which he is bound - he shall pay unto the last jot and tittle for his every act - be it Mercy or Violence! I say- like unto the Act - so the Judgement - so the Payment! There is No hiding Place! I say it is more merciful to drown thine self than to caught up in the Web of this begetting of offspring for sensuous purposes I say to transgress the Law is to Reap the Reward - So let it be said that the Energy so misused shall be Transmuted and therein is another story.

I say they shall Come to Know that which I say to be True - and for their own sake - So let it be said that the ones which misuse the Sacred Rites of Procreation - and goes within the bed of Another thoughtless of his Sacred Rites! "The Sacred Rites", shall come to answer for his Unknowing - for his misdirected energy - for in this case there is no necessity to speak at length on the Law -- Let it suffice that the Law shall require of him the full Payment of Every Act - Every Deed - So be it I have Spoken and I shall speak Again - for this is Mine Day and I shall have Mine Say!

So be it I AM Sananda

Recorded by Sister Thedra of the Emerald Cross

...Know Why Such Secrecy

Beloved Ones - When it is given unto thee to see the Whole of the Plan ye shall then Know why there has been such Secrecy - for I say unto thee it is necessary to guard well the Parts - for the Parts are so well Guarded that None shall be lost or destroyed -- While the Candidate for the Great initiation may fail - and be cast aside and be forgotten - there shall be another which shall be raised up to take his place -- While I say unto thee each has a part - and no part is ever lost yet the parts shall be put together to make up the "Whole" - I say the plan is Perfect -

Complete within itself -- While the Candidate shall Make Fit himself to serve within the Plan - and when this is done he shall not be denied.

While I say: "Many are called and Few are Chosen" - it is for them to hear the "Call" and present them self - and when they are found trustworthy and Prepared they are then given a Part which shall prepare them for yet Greater Responsibility and as they are prepared, So Do they receive.

Now let it be said that As they are Prepared, So do they Receive - for I say: they are not alone - neither are they forgotten by the Mighty Host - they are watched with the Utmost Care - from the time they ask to serve until they have <u>Attained</u> - or until they have been placed within the compound wherein there are others which shall give unto them that which they are <u>Willing</u> to accept - or prepared to receive --

Now let this be understood - that each has his place which he has Made for Himself - he Creates his Own environment therefore he is the partaker of his Own Creation and environment --

Yet when he sickens of his own Creation he can turn from it and Withdraw his energy from it and give it no more substance - and for this it shall become as nought for his is a World created by thought. His is a World of "Illusion" and when the Illusion is seen for that which it is - it is no longer, it becomes NO THING - it is dissolved in thought and form as the droplets of dew in the sun --

For this do I say be ye mindful of thine words for they shall bless thee or curse -- for they are held within the thought world and given form - And there are men which Know Not that they have created their own "Hell". Yet they refuse to Accept that which they have Created: It is said "They shall father their own Child" be he Saint or Sinner, for they Are Responsible for their own creation. So be it the Law -- I say unto them: be ye Aware of that which ye Create for thou dost Create by every living breath - every word - every act - let it be for thine own sake that ye become Aware of Thine Part in the Creation of the New World which shall become thine Inheritance for thou shall live in the World which thou hast Created - So let it be for thine Own Generation that they too might partake of the Greater Glory -- So be it I have spoken unto them which have an ear to hear - Let <u>them</u> hear, for the deaf shall not hear neither shall they be as ones prepared to receive Me or of Me. So be it I Am One sent that they might be prepared for the Greater Part - the Great Learning --

I AM thine Older Brother and thine Sibor - Berean

Recorder - Sister Thedra of the Emerald Cross

Christ-Mass

Be ye as mine hand made manifest, and say unto them as I would - that I am come - come into the Earth that there be Light. So shall it be - while it is given unto me to be the risen Lord - and the Light of the world, I say unto them I am the Son of God sent that they be brought out of bondage.

Let it be said that the Lord thy God hast come this day - and what hast he found? They are as ones eating, drinking, and making merry - drunken on new wine. Singing, laughing, as ones drunken - knowing not their own identity, yet they claim that they know me - the "Risen

Lord" - I say unto thee: Oh ye fools! I come not that ye be justified in thine foolishness. I come not that ye put thine fingers into mine wounds. I have said never again shall ye open mine wounds that ye might put thine fingers therein. I say it is finished!

Too I say ye shall shake off the old and put on the new! No more shall ye burn the midnite oil - that ye make merry the birth of a babe - I say ye shall now arise and give ye thanks that I am now as one fully prepared to lead thee out of bondage. Yet, I bid thee arise, Come follow ye me, turn from thine puny way and leave thine paint and tinsel and see ye that which I shall do - for I shall show thee greater things than thou hast dreamed of. I say unto thee thou hast not seen that which I shall do - for I shall show mine hand to the just and the prudent, and ye shall be as ones blest.

I say unto thee turn from thine childish ways and come follow ye me and I shall show thee many things which thou hast not seen. So be it and I am the Lord thy God Come that ye might have Light.

Abide therein and be ye blest.

I Am Sananda, Son of the Most High Living God.

Recorded by Sister Thedra of the Emerald Cross

Christ Speaks of the Anti-Christ - Selfish Customs - Selfless Service

While it is come that many are preparing for the festive table the word which ye shall be given for them shall be recorded thusly - it shall be given unto them as it is given unto thee - not one word shall be changed or taken away, nothing added to - then they shall do that which they will with them.

Be it so that this season of the year brings much gladness to the hearts of the little ones which knows not the meaning thereof - Yet to the ones which suffer from the cold, from hunger, want, and from disease of many kinds, they are the ones which for the most part are forgotten in thy running hither and yon that ye might satisfy thine own desire - and comply to the custom of man.

Now I say, the gifts which are brought to the Christ is not the tinsel and the furbish - which is given in these days of thine "hypocrisy". These are an abomination in mine sight - these are of the "AntiChrist". These are not of the Christ!

For it is prompted by desire of Self - it is not selfless service! I say the SELFLESS Service, the giving of SELF - is the greater gift - the ONE which is acceptable - it is said that the gold, the frankincense and myrrh are but symbols of the gift of selfless service - and it is given unto thee to be selfish in thine giving -

To whom givest thou? To them in need?

To them which suffer?

To them which hunger?

To them which serve me?

Mine servants which serve thee?

I say these are forgotten in thine rush, thine haste to make festive thine own board - in thine "merry-making". I say ye sing thine songs to whom? To what, the "Babe"? Ye are so foolish! As the babe in the cradle, ye know not the meaning of this season.

For it is the time of the Solstice, when the great orb of thy Sun moves back on its cycle to the South from the North, and then on its course - well-ordered course - and the pagans worshipped the Sun - these knew more of the meaning of this season than the so-called "Christians", for they have not been enlightened in these things - I say it is a time of observation, watchfulness, and sobriety. It is a time of fulfilling - a time of bringing forth, a time of great rest, a period of dormancy, and it is not the day for which to "Make Merry".

As for the "Babe", the Babe - now mature of stature - gentle of heart, strong of arm - wise beyond thine concept, stands with hand poised in position to give his benediction upon all which ask of Him this day! He is no longer the "Babe" in swaddling clothes!

I ask of thee wherein is thine comprehension - by what customs art thou bound? I say cut loose thine leg-irons, turn from thine puny ways and seek out the Christ - make ye haste to enlighten thineself - and nothing shall be hidden from them which seek in the Light of the Christ they shall find.

So be it I am He that which hast spoken unto thee of the greater things - Let it be understood I am not bound by Earth, flesh, neither law of Earth, or for that matter no law binds me, I AM free - Be ye as One with Me this day - Make no mockery by thine own imagery and be ye as ones prepared to receive me and of me.

I am the Lord thy God known in the realms of Light as

Sananda

Recorded by Sister Thedra of the Emerald Cross

Look! See!

Mine Beloved ones: I speak unto this day that they might know that which I say unto them for 'they' are as ones which have their fingers in their ears - their hands before their eyes. They hear not and neither do they see! While I say unto them: "Look! See! Know ye that it is now come that I am returned and for this have ye waited, I say I am come!" I am come as a thief in the night - I have found them slumbering, and I have found thee eating and drinking and making merry - fortune thineself that which I come to give unto thee, for I foresee that which shall come upon the Earth, and the peoples thereof.

I say unto thee great sorrow shall come to the peoples of all the lands and they shall lay aside their weapons of war and seek food, for their bellies shall be empty and their heart shall be filled with sorrow for there shall be great suffering.

I say this day has long been prophesied, and foretold as of old - yet they have given unto themself credit for being wise. I say poor foolish mortals which knoweth not from whence cometh their strength, I say poor foolish mortals! Let thine eyes be opened and take thine fingers from out thine ears and hear ye that which I say unto thee - I have set forth the law which shall be unto thee sufficient, and I have declared unto thee the way of the Lord is straight and narrow - ye shall walk therein. Ye shall not deviate from the law - Ye shall be as ones prepared to enter into mine place of abode - How do I prepare? thou hast asked. I say unto thee: Ye shall apply thineself, ye shall apply the law unto thine ownself - Ye shall obey the law and at no time shall ye deny the Lord thy God - for I am come that ye be delivered up, that ye be brought out of bondage - Know ye that thou art bound and no man shall bring thee out against thine own will!

I say unto thee man is not thine salvation, his word is not sufficient unto thine salvation, neither his preachment nor his good words - I say his good works are not sufficient unto thy salvation - it is <u>thineself</u> thou art responsible for, thine own self! No man can atone for thine misused energy, for thine actions.

Now let it be said: That thou art responsible unto the law, and no man shall atone for thee. Ye shall atone for thine own misused energy! Let this be remembered - ask no man his opinion for by them shall ye be bound - I say unto thee free thineself of all thine opinions, thine preconceived ideas and be ye as one blest. Let no man trip thee up. There are ones which would!

I say unto thee be ye alert and know ye that there is none so foolish as the one which thinks himself wise - none so sad as he which betrays himself. I speak that ye might hear me,

So be it - I am the Lord thy God.

Recorded by Sister Thedra of the Emerald Cross

They Need the Experience

Beloved of Mine Being: Be ye blest this day and give unto them this Word and let it be known that which I say unto thee for this do I give This Word unto thee! --

When it is Come that they shall be scattered unto the winds they shall cry out and ask for Assistance - Yet it is the Law that they first Ask for assistance -- They shall be as ones prepared to Receive it - then they shall be as ones which have prepared them self and they shall be as ones which Know Wherein they are Staid - for no man can tell them that which they shall See - Do - or Experience --

Now when they have need of Such Experience We of the Host shall not deny them - for it is theirs and it shall be profitable unto them - Yet I say they shall Cry and Ask of Man Assistance - and they shall deny that We - the Host exists - And these shall come to Know that We Come Not to confuse them or to give unto them Bread Alone - Rather that they might have Light and be prepared for the Greater Part - When it is given unto them to lay down their Arms and turn from their Hatred - their Guilt - their Willful way - We shall give unto them that which We have for them - Then they shall Know the Power of the Word - And they shall Know how to Use It --

So be it this is Mine Word this day ---

So be it and Selah ---

I AM Sananda

Sanandas Answer to Their Bitter Cup

Beloved Ones: While it is yet time let it be said that there are ones which would belittle Mine Word and give unto thee the bitter cup - Yet I say they shall drink of the Cup which they prepare for thee - for have I not set up This House? - This Temple have I prepared - and I have founded it upon the "Rock Which I AM" -- So be it that ye shall be as Ones Prepared for yet Greater Things - for I have said that ye shall drink of "Mine Cup" and it shall be Sweet Indeed -- Let not that which they have prepared for thee touch thine lips - for I say therein they have put their own poison which they shall partake of - They shall drink their own bitters and it shall be unto them their Own Responsibility --

For I say unto thee it shall be of no concern unto thee - for I Am thy Shield and thy Buckler -- So be it I Am Responsible for MINE OWN WORDS and it shall be given unto them as they are given unto thee -- So be it that I am Unmoved by their Wanton and their words which Are Not of Me neither are they of the Light -- I say they ARE NOT OF THE LIGHT.

I AM the Lord thy God - Sananda

Recorded by Sister Thedra of the Emerald Cross

Swift Changes
Sorry Generation

Beloved of My Being: Hear ye that which I say unto thee - It is given unto Me to be thine Eternal Mother - and for this I say unto thee: It is the day wherein ye shall stand upon the High Holy Mount and witness that which shall come about by Natural Law - And it shall be given unto thee to see Great and Swift Changes within the Earth - and the heavens thereabouts for it is the Day of Swift Change -- Mighty Changes shall be brought about within the twinkling of an eye - yet no man Knoweth the exact hour - Let it be said that many shall be unprepared - Yet it is given unto Me to See them when they are so unmindful of their Inheritance - and know not that they are given a part in a Great Plan --

Yet I reach out Mine Hand and I put it forth as a Mother that they Might have Light and know that they Are Not of the "Sorry Generation" I say that they shall divide themself - some shall be prepared - some shall be Unprepared and these shall be the sorry ones - pitiful shall be their lot - Yet I have held them within Mine Heart that they Might Come into Maturity and fulfillment -- It is said this is the Day of Fulfillment.- It Is Truly So.

Yet for the rebellious, they shall wait - and it shall be long and hard.

Mine Hand I extend and Mine Strength is Abundant - Mine Love Knows no bounds - Yet they have Not the mind to accept the fullness of their inheritance --

Let it be said: They too shall <u>Come</u> to Know - Weary not for they are slow in their Awakening and it is given unto them to begin to Stir - Concern Not thyself for the rebellious for they but deter thee and it shall be given unto thee to feed the hungry first - and last - And give unto them that which We give unto thee for them and let them choose as they Will -- This is the Word which I have for thee this Day -- So be it I AM thine Mother Eternal

To Become is the Hope...

Beloved Ones: Were it not for the Grace of Our Father there would be no Day - No Night - No Communication - No Work No Rest - No Blessings -- Behold ye this day the Gifts which He has bestowed upon Us - The Gift of Spirit - Life Eternal And the Inheritance which He has Willed unto Us --

For this I say Praise ye the Name of Solen Aum Solen -- Forever - and Forever -- Harken unto Him and be ye as One with Him - and be ye as One Prepared for thine Inheritance which He has so Graciously Prepared for thee --

Let it be given unto thee to be prepared - and for this do We the Host Standby to give assistance -- Let it be said that As ye are Prepared So shall ye Receive --

Let it be said: That to Know is Wisdom. - And to Be is the Greater Part - for to Become is the Hope of All the Aspirants - yet to <u>Know</u> is given unto the Initiate --

Then he Becomes That which he Hoped to Become -- The Being is the Attainment -- We come that ye Might Attain unto thy Goodhood - in Him Our Father shall it be - for this is thine Inheritance -- So be it I am Come that ye might have Light --

I AM Sananda

Flesh is Bound by the Law of Earth

Beloved Ones: Let it be established this day that there is No Limitations in Spirit - Spirit is Limitless and Knows No Limitations - I say that the Spirit is FREE - And Is Not Bound by Flesh -

Flesh is bound - bound by the Law of Earth - Earth Law - and the flesh is limited by its law under which it has its being, the form of flesh is limited for in Spirit the law of Earth is as Nothing for it is Over Come, Transcended and holds No Power over the Spirit -- It is now come when ye shall come to Know that thou Art Not bound by the LAW OF FLESH - thou art Not Bound by flesh, neither its law --

While it is so - there are certain Conditions under which thou art bound - by thine own preconceived ideas – opinions, thine own will - and by the opinions of others which thou hast Accepted!

Now it is said: "Be ye as Ones freed from All thine legirons" and let not thine preconceived ideas - opinions - trip thee up - Come ye unto Me and I shall lead thee Out of Bondage -- And it is So; So it shall be.-

I say unto thee: I Know thee - I Know from whence thou Came - and I Know Whither thou Goest - So be it that I am the One sent to Assist thee and I am Not bound by man's law, his Opinions - Creeds - Dogmas - Long hast he been within the net of his own weaving - So be it that he shall now Come to Know the weaving is his own and he shall learn how to extricate himself - Yet he shall have OUR Assistance when he is so prepared to Receive it - We are not so foolish as to impose upon him or his free will -- It is said: As he is Prepared so shall he Receive - So it is - So shall it be --

Let it be understood that there are ones which have prepared themself for to receive Us and of Us - these shall be glad for their preparation - So be it I am One sent that ye be Prepared -- For this have I given of Mineself --

I AM the Lord thy God

Sananda

Recorded by Sister Thedra of the Emerald Cross

The Plan Unfolds

Blessed Ones: While I say unto thee it is Mine Part to bring unto thee this Word - I say it is thine to receive it and it shall be for the Good of all - Let no man tell thee that thou art as Nothing - of no consequence, for I tell thee thou Art part of the Great and Mighty Plan which is unfolding before thee - Let it be said that One shall come and he shall bring with him another and he shall have within his hand the Power to bring thee forth - Yet he shall be as One Silent And he shall be as One Gentle - Silent concerning his Authority and Power - Yet I say he has such Power for he has earned it - He has proven himself trustworthy and he shall not betray himself --

He shall be as one of flesh and bone even unto the last part of him.- he shall walk and talk as man and he shall be as man And he shall be as the One which hast come and gone and he shall leave with thee a gift of small value - yet it shall be unto thee a talisman and ye shall be as one blest by him for he shall bless thee with his presence - While he shall not linger as he has a Great Mission, I say he shall not tarry - So be ye as one prepared to receive him - Receive him as a Brother for I say unto thee - I have vouchsafed for him for I know him - Be ye blest to receive him and of him --

I AM thine Sibor And thine Older Brother

Sanat Kumara

The Word Hast Been Spoken Let it be Perfect

Behold the Hand of God - See it Move - See the Perfection of the Movement for it shall be given unto thee to See - and to Know the Perfect Action thereof for It Moves according unto the Will of the Father - for He is the Giver of All "Perfect" manifestation and it shall be the "Perfect Manifestation" - At No time shall the Hand of God be held in Abeyance for the Word hast been Spoken "Let there Be Perfection in the Manifestation" And it shall be - For this was the Word Spoken - LET IT BE PERFECT!

Ye shall behold that Perfection and Know that it is the Will of the Father brought into Manifestation -- So be it I have Spoken and thou hast heard Me. So be it that I AM the Lord thy God -

Sananda

Recorded by Sister Thedra of the Emerald Cross

I Supplicate Before Them
Sananda

Most Holy and Perfect Father - Giver and Taker of Life - for thou art the 'All' - O, Father of us all, be it so that these thine sons become aware of the fullness of their inheritance. Their Light which is thine, which is endowed them through and by thy grace - I speak unto thee Father that they might come to know that they are thine Sons with the power and the authority to speak unto thee as I have - that thou hearest them even as thou hast heard me.

Cause them to hear me that they might come to know thee as I know thee. Father, O Blessed Father, I come before them in supplication that their hearts might be softened, and that they might be quickened and know that thou hast heard.

Father, for thine mercy this hast been made possible - Yet they know only in part, yet they know not the fullness of thine love - that which thou hast given unto them as their inheritance - Be it so Father, that they are thine Sons which sleep within flesh.

I say unto them Awaken! Mine word hast gone out from mine mouth, Let Them Awaken! And become alive and know that there is a place prepared for them and that they have a time and a place. Let the time of sleep be finished and the time of awakening be this day that they might return unto thee with me. So be it Father that we, thine sons sent that they be brought, shall await the great day of awakening!

So be it a great day of rejoicing! Let it be as thou hast willed - All praise unto Thee - All the Glory is Thine, Father.

So shall it ever Be, worlds without end.

I am thine Son - Sananda

Recorded by Sister Thedra of the Emerald Cross

Forewarning

Be ye as Ones Alert for I say unto thee there shall be Protests and Oppositions -- There shall be Whisperings and Mutterings - and they shall bear such fruit that shall bring forth much bitterness - And the thorns from the fruit shall tear the flesh of the creators - I say the creators of such fruit, such bitterness, shall have their flesh torn by such thorns as shall be unto them much pain - much suffering - Let not thine hand be pricked! Let not their creation touch thee -- For I say unto thee: they which prepare the <u>bitter</u> <u>portion</u> for thee shall drink thereof and they shall Know that it IS of their own concoction - and they shall be as ones which shall bear the burden thereof!

So let it be said No one escapes the Law - So be it this is Mine Word unto thee this day -- I am Come that ye might Know that Which Goes On About Thee

I AM

These Shall I Touch
Sananda

Behold the Hand of God, See it Move - And Know ye that the Works which I do shall be According unto the Will of the Father which hast

Sent Me - And at no time shall I betray Mine Trust -- I say Behold the Hand of God - See It Move - and Know it to be the Will of the Father which hast sent Me.

Now Ye shall be as ones Prepared to Receive the Word which shall be for them which have ears to hear and a mind to learn - And they shall bear witness of Mine Word for they shall Know them to be valid - And these I shall touch and they shall be lifted up - And not one shall be overlooked or forgotten - I say each one is observed and he has been given that which should be Sufficient --

Yet I say they are weak of Spirit - and are as ones Asleep on their feet - they are fearful and have little comprehension of the "Great Plan" which slowly unfolds before them - I say I am Come that they might have comprehension - yet they are Satisfied with their well set – well-worn opinions; they are as ones "Self-Centered" and give no Credit unto the Ones which KNOW, for they are as yet in darkness - they but THINK! They are the thinkers - So be it that I am Come that they might know even as I - When they have ridden themself of their Thinking - their Self-Created State - I shall cause them to Know - and they shall <u>Then</u> See the foolishness of their own puny ways - for I say I am Come that they have Light - that they might Know even as I --

Now it is clearly stated that there is a Mighty Host and They Are thine Benefactors - They Are the Emissaries sent forth from the "Inner Temple" that ye of Earth be lifted up - that ye might Know - Yet I say they fear that which they know not they are not prepared to receive the fullness of the Plan - they See it Not! Yet they THINK themself Wise!

When it is Come that they are brought into the place wherein I am they shall be as ones WISER! Yet they shall be as ones humble - and be as ones which Know - They shall not strut themself - neither shall they be as the foolish! I say there is No Foolishness in the Mighty Host! They are about the Father's Business - So be it I have said Mine Say -- Let it suffice them that I am Come that they be lifted up --

So be it and Selah

I AM

Opposition
I have Instructed Thee

While it is yet time, let it be said that they which rebel against the Plan and "The Word" shall wait and they shall be as ones unprepared to receive Me and of Me - While I say they which have <u>heard</u> that which I say shall be as ones which shall receive Me and of Me - for they shall be as ones which have put from them All rebellion - and All pity and willfulness - They shall be of the Peace which is Mine - and they shall not be in Any way whatsoever a fortune unto themself - I say they shall be Selfless in their Service and they shall serve Joyfully and with the GREATEST of JOY shall they Serve - They shall ask of no man for his opinion - or for verification for they shall KNOW and therein is Wisdom - Now ye shall be reminded that there Are ones which would trip thee up - yet ye shall be as ones prepared - that ye put not thine foot into their trap - their web - I say they have been well baited and placed within the places wherein ye least suspect - and at no time shall ye be caught off guard - Remember well The Way of the Initiate, for it is the Law by which ye shall live and attain thine Victory - I say ye shall at all times remember that which I have said! For I have given unto thee the Law - and Instructed thee in "The Way of The Initiate" for the Initiate has Attained unto the Height - And he knows -

Yet the Candidate hast only aspired unto the Height and he has Not as yet Attained his Illumination - he has Not as yet entered into the "Inner Temple" he but Aspires unto the Greater Learning - While I say ye are given that which ye are prepared to receive - Let it be the Greater Part - For this Am I Come - Let it Suffice that I Am the Priest Within this Temple -

I AM Sananda -

Recorded by Sister Thedra of the Emerald Cross

The Administrators

"Sweet" is the Word – "Power" is the Word - for there IS Power in the Word - for It is that Which brings into manifestation the things of the Seen world -- All thine seen world is brought into manifestation through the Spoken Word --

And for this hast thou been enabled to enjoy that which ye take so Lightly - without thought - For it is given unto Me to see them take their "daily bread" as if it were their creation and their rightful portion giving No thought from whence cometh the "daily bread" --

While they Do go into the places wherein they say "Give us" - as the parrot - Knowing not the Energy or the Word - Neither do they know the Source of that which is their lot - portion --

Their wants they make known unto them about them - Yet I say unto them - The Administrators of their Inheritance are Well Aware of their needs - And I say that the Administrators are not in the least moved by their "Wants" for they are many - colored by their own preconceived ideas - likes and dislikes - by their own tastes and distastes - by their own <u>thinking</u> --

While I say the Council Knows Well their needs -- And for this do We Administer unto them according unto their Needs - that they might Grow in Stature - That they might GROW into MATURITY - and be Responsible for themself - for their Inheritance --

THEN they shall be given <u>IN</u> <u>FULL</u> --

So be it that I have said much of "Inheritance" - Yet be there one amongst thee which Knows the Fullness thereof? I say thou hast Not received it - Thou hast not the Memory of it -- Yet ye shall be given that which hast been held in trust for thee - for it Is held in trust for thee for the day of thine return --

So be it that thine Inheritance is of the Greatest Concern unto Me -

The Lord thy God -

Sananda

Recorded by Sister Thedra of the Emerald Cross

Parts of the Plan...
None So Vital as the One I Hold
Sananda

Behold in Me the Son of God - The Light of the World -- And be ye as one prepared to receive of Me - For it is Now Come when I shall reveal unto thee many things hitherto Unknown -- Let it be said that the Parts shall be added together and they shall be as One Design - One Pattern which shall be Part of the Plan -- I say the parts shall fit together and they shall make up the <u>Whole</u> --

So be it that there Are many Parts - Yet none are so Vital as the One <u>I</u> <u>hold</u> - For I hold within Mine Hand the whole of the Plan - And I know it - Wherein I have served long and tirelessly -- I Am Aware of All the Parts - and without One Part the Plan would not be complete -- So be it that thou hast a Part and ye shall not discount it - Ye shall not discount <u>One</u> <u>Part</u> --

While I say should <u>one</u> fail <u>in</u> <u>his</u> <u>part</u> another shall be raised up to fill the place wherein he failed -- The part which hast been given unto thee hast been a Gift which thou hast earned - by the Law of Divine Right - and thou hast been the Inheritors of the Law - For thou hast the Law by which thou shall extricate thine own self from the web of thine own creation - from the world of Illusion -- For this have I Come that ye might Know the Law -- I do not interpret the Law - I reveal it - and it is thine part to abide thereby -- So be it that there are none so foolish as to betray their trust - for they are the traitors -- Let it be said that they are the saddest of the lot.

I Am Come that ye

Might Know the Law --

So be it I AM

Sananda

Recorded by Sister Thedra of the Emerald Cross

The Precious Gifts Shall Not Be Pilfered

Beloved of Mine Being - It is Now Come when there shall be a Great and Glorious Manifestation of the Power which shall be used to Glorify the Father Which hast Sent Me -- I say that there shall be Great and Glorious Manifestations of the Power which IS And None shall pilfer that which is the Gift of Mine Servants -- I say that the Power which is the Precious Gift bestowed upon Mine Servants shall not be misused or pilfered -- It shall be as the Shield and the Buckler and they which are of Mine Fold shall be blest –

They shall be As Ones Blest! -- For I shall Bless them -- For it is Mine Part to Know that which Goes On -- I Know the wheat from the chaff - I Know that there are ones amongst thee which wear sheep clothing -- So be it that I Am Not of a mind to be Put Out - I Am Not of a mind to be Put Off -- For I say I shall wage war on them which do use Mine Name in <u>vain</u> -- So let it Suffice that I AM the Lord thy God.

Sananda

Thou Hast Come to Do This Now

Beloved Ones - When it is come that thou art free from All bondage - Ye shall Know as I Know, and for this do ye now wait.

While I say - Be ye as ones prepared for the Greater Part, I say <u>this</u> is thine preparation - for <u>this</u> is the day - the time - the place of thine preparation -- And when thou hast passed from this place - this time - thou shall find that thou hast either failed in thine part - Or - Thou hast Won the Victory! For this is the Time of <u>Action</u> - When No man stands still - And when no man finds himself without Some Part within the Plan as a Whole - for All are included - And as for the "Great and Divine Plan" - There is No Time - Yet thou hast been given a Part - and that Part is NO SMALL PART -- While thou but consider it a small part - Let it be said - It is that for which thou hast come into embodiment for to do - Be ye as Ones Alert - and falter not - for I see thee waver and sicken -- And as far as the part which thou hast - I say it is the Fulfillment of thine Covenant - made so long ago -- So be it that it is given unto Me to See and Know - For I AM

The Lord thy God -- I AM Sananda

Recorded by Sister Thedra of the Emerald Cross

Ones to Follow the One Which Has Come

Beloved Ones -- Wherein is it said that One shall Come unto thee bearing a gift - and ye shall receive it in Mine Name -- For it shall be given unto him to be One Sent -- He shall bring another with him and he shall say unto thee that he has come for the purpose of learning --

So it shall be - Yet he knows that which he comes for to do -- For his coming shall be beneficial unto All - for he knows that which goes on in the world of man - he is alert - and at no time shall ye fear that which goes on - For I say nothing shall Stay thine hand -- Nothing shall deter thine hand - for thine hand shall be Mine hand - and it shall be swift to do Mine Work -- Let it be understood that there are ones which would beset thee and destroy thine Work for the sake of glorifying self -- For this do I say be ye alert - for He cometh swiftly -- Be ye as one prepared to receive him - and be ye as one alert - for he cometh as man as flesh and blood -- Let it be understood that He is One of Mine Messengers - Be ye One with him for it is Now Come when there shall be Great Revelation and He shall be part of it -- So be it and Selah ---

I AM Come that ye might Know --

So be it - I AM Sananda

Recorded by Sister Thedra of the Emerald Cross

Flesh and Spirit

Beloved Ones -- This day I would say unto thee - The Way is clear before thee and the day is Now Come when ye shall See that which hast been hidden from thine sight -- For I say unto thee - Thine eyes shall be opened - and thine Spirit shall be quickened - and ye shall Know - and Know that ye Know. It is given unto Me to see thee as thou art -- Yet thou hast the veil about thee - and ye but <u>think</u> thineself bound in flesh -- While I say flesh can not bind thee longer -- When it is come that thou hast broken the bonds which now bind thee - Ye shall never again go into bondage - for ye shall stand as ones Victorious over flesh.- While I say "Ye shall no longer be bound by flesh" - let it be understood that thou Art Not to despise the flesh - neither resist it - for it is thy vehicle of expression within the world of form -- It is that which is given unto thee to use as thine Earthly Vehicle of expression. While I say "Flesh cannot hold thee bound," I too say that ye shall step from thine vehicle of flesh - free - to go into bondage no more -- When it is come that thine Mission is Complete - finished - Ye shall step forth as One in shining Armor and ye shall not want -- Ye shall be as ones free forever -- So be it that I have Spoken unto thee of the flesh - and of the Spirit -- Let it be said that ye have been as ones prepared for to receive Me and that which I have for thee -- Yet ye shall be Alert -- Let no man trip thee up - for it is said "There are ones amongst thee which would". So be it I Am Come that thine feet be firmly planted upon the "Rock" which I AM -- I shall not deceive thee or mislead thee --

I AM Sananda - the Son of God

Recorded by Sister Thedra of the Emerald Cross

THE SLEEPERS DO NOT HEAR

Behold! See that which shall be done in the time allotted unto thee -- For a Mighty Work shall be done - and it behooves Me to make known that which is Going On -- For it is the time of Awakening - and the day draws nigh when ye shall See and Know that the time is Come - When the Mighty Host hast drawn Close - And they which make up the Host hast given of Themself that they be part of the Host -- And it is Mine Part to be the Host of the Host -- Host of Hosts Am I - For this do I say unto thee I Am the Lord of Hosts - I Am the Lord God - Sent of Mine Father that there be Light - And that there be a Great Awakening amongst the Sleepers -- Now I say the sleepers are like unto the <u>dead</u> - they are not aware of their sleep -- They are Not Aware of their Source of Being - They are as ones dead -- for they neither Know from whence they came or whither they goeth -- I bid them Awaken! Arise! Come Alive! And be up and about the Fathers business --

Yet they hear Not!

While I Speak the Word they sleep --

Yet the Word hast gone out from Mine mouth - which shall fall upon fertile Soil - and they shall quicken the Spirit and bring forth that which is ready -- For I say not all shall respond unto "The Word". So be it they shall awaken in another day - another place - at another time. Yet I say: "Blest are they which Awaken this day" -- So be it I AM Come that they be blest - That they Awaken --

So be it I AM Sananda --

Recorded by Sister Thedra of the Emerald Cross

I am the Portal....

Blest art thou O Mine Children - For thou art Mine Children born of Me Art Thou -- It is Mine Part to remind thee of thine Inheritance for thou art prone to forgetfulness -- I speak Not that I might remind Mineself - I speak that <u>Ye</u> be reminded - that ye be Awakened unto thine true Identity --

Thou hast Not remembered ME "The Mother" from which thou hast gone forth -- I Am the Portal through which thou hast come -- For there is None Other through which thou can come - Thou hast none other means by which thou canst take form -- I say that I Am the Portal through thou hast come and there is none other through which thou canst take form.

While I Am "The Mother" I Am The Father - for the Father and I are ONE ---

When it is given unto thee to Know Me thine Mother thou shall also Know the Father for He and I are ONE ---

When it is come that ye are free from All thine bondage - ye shall know as I Know - and for this have I reminded thee of the Oneness which WE share ---

Let it be said that Mine Children shall return unto Me and they shall be as ones returned from a Long and troubled Sleep and I shall no more remember their Sleep - their Waywardness - for I Know them and I Am a loving Mother as well as a Merciful ONE --

Keep thine hand in Mine and I shall lead thee and comfort thee and give unto thee that which thou hast need of ---

So be it that I await thine Return -- And Great shall be thine Joy.

I AM Thine Mother Eternal

> **Recorded by Sister Thedra of the Emerald Cross**

Preparedness is the Fulfilling of the Plan

Beloved Ones - With this WORD I shall bless thee - And for this is it given - It is the Part for which thou hast waited -- Now ye shall be as ones which hast thine hand in Mine - and I shall lead thee - I say I shall lead thee - And it is given unto Me to be One with Mine Father which hast Sent Me --

So be it that I AM the Lord thy God and it is Mine Part to give unto thee as thou Can Bear It - As thou art Prepared to Receive -- When it is come that ye are Prepared - I shall give unto thee thine Inheritance in Full -- And I Am the Guardian of It - thine Inheritance -- Yet I say - It is not yet come that thou art Prepared to Receive it - for the Glory of It thou could Not bear -- While it is given unto Me to See thee weep for the darkness - and for thine own faults - and short-comings - I say it is not sufficient - it is not enough - for it is given unto Me to Know wherein thou art lacking - wherein thou dost fall short - and too - It behooves Me to point out thine own shortcomings - For this is thine own Fortune that thou art Accumulating - and it shall either be thine VICTORY - or thine downfall - While I Am Come to Point the Way I can but lead - and give unto thee that which ye can bear -- It is not lawful that I betray Mine trust - for I am not a traitor -- I Am Not Come to mislead thee - I give unto thee no promises that I am not prepared to fulfill - For it is Mine Part to give unto thee As ye can Bear it - as thou art Prepared to Receive.

Now this "Preparedness" is the <u>thing</u> - To Be or - Not to Be - For <u>This</u> is the Whole of the Plan - To Prepare thineself for to Return unto thine Rightful Place - Thine Own Source wherein All things are Known. So be it that I Am the Lord thy God - And I Am the Lord of Hosts - The Host Which hast been Prepared to Assist in this day - In this Plan - And in thine Ascent --

So be ye as One with Me and Rejoice Forever More!

I AM Sananda

Recorded by Sister Thedra of the Emerald Cross

Anti-Christs & Traitors
These are the Ones

Host of Hosts AM I -- I say unto thee: - The Host of Hosts AM I - I speak unto thee in thine own tongue - that ye might comprehend that which I say unto thee -- While I <u>Give</u> unto thee that which is for the Good of All - it is not understood by the ones which yet sleepeth -- I say they which sleep have not the mind to comprehend that which I say unto thee -- Yet it is given unto Me to Know them and their wont -- It is Mine Part to give unto them as though they were Alert -- When the Word has gone forth from Mine mouth it is for anyone - anywhere - that has a mind to learn - to receive it -- And therein ends Mine responsibility unto them ---

Yet let it be understood - that I stand by as One prepared to give of Mine Self - when they Ask of Me - Then I Am allowed by Law to give as I give unto thee -- When it is come that they have prepared themself for to receive Me - I shall Come in and give unto them that which I have kept for them. They know Not that I Am prepared to give unto them their Inheritance in Full - So be it that I Am Come that they might awaken - yet I Know some shall sleep overtime and be as ones unprepared -- These are the Anti-Christs - these are the traitors -- These are the ones which shall cry out "My Lord! My Lord! have you forsaken me?" These are the ones which wait for 'Signs and Wonders' - these are the ones which run hither and yon seeking verification - these are the ones which betray themself and deny ME -- These are the ones which have Slept while I walk among them - these are the ones which have thought themself Wise! - These are the foolish ones which shall be caught up short of their course -- So be it I say unto them - Sleep on ye sleepers - sleep on -- Ye shall find thine Own way hard and long - for I shall withdraw Mine hand and remove Mineself -- So be it as ye Will it ---

I Am Come that All might have Light --

So be it I AM the Lord thy God

Sananda

Recorded by Sister Thedra of the Emerald Cross

Famine

Beloved Ones -- The time is come to alert them -- and ye shall say unto them as I would say - That the time draws nigh when there shall be Great Fire from beneath the soil - which shall parch the surface of the ground -- And it shall yield no vegetation thereupon -- And there shall be Great Suffering among the people - and they shall lay aside their weapons of destruction to search for food --

I speak unto thee as One which Sees that which shall come upon them because of their own willfulness - and rebellion -- I see the results thereof -- While it is Mine Part to say unto them - "Turn from thine own willful ways and seek the Light" It is as though they are <u>determined</u> to destroy themself -- I say man is the result of his own will - and he hast Willed his own downfall -- While I say he is the result of his own will.- I speak of that which he sees about him - and the condition about him for he has made - or created his own hell - his own environment - the world in which he finds himself -- It is truly the world of man -- For the Father hast never Willed it thus - I say the Father hast <u>never</u> willed it thus. While it is come that they rush headlong into destruction - I say they shall be reminded of their own responsibility and they shall learn that they Alone are responsible for their own Acts - Actions - and it is for this that I say unto them - Be ye as one prepared to follow where I lead thee - and ask of no man his opinion - or blessing - for I bid thee Come - Follow ye Me - and I shall Lead thee out of bondage --

Seek ye the Light - and no man shall take from thee thine Inheritance --

I say unto thee Seek ye the Light which I AM - and I shall lead thee out of bondage --

So be it I Am Come that ye might have Light ---

I AM Sananda

Recorded by Sister Thedra of the Emerald Crossinn

I Say: Let them Know the Meaning of Peace

Beloved Ones -- The way is now made clear before thee - And it is given unto Me to See and to Know - for I Am the Lord thy God - Come unto thee that Ye might be prepared to enter into the Holy of Holies - Wherein there is no darkness. So be it that I Am given unto waiting - Yet I say unto thee the time is come when I shall go out amongst them. And I shall openly declare war on the <u>unjust</u> and the <u>imprudent</u> -- And for this do I say unto thee I come not to bring <u>Peace</u> I Am Come that the <u>Way</u> <u>be</u> <u>made</u> <u>for</u> <u>Peace</u> -- I say - They which do oppress Mine people - and give unto Mine Prophets the bitter cup shall be as ones which have thrown over-board their own life belt -- And they shall see the folly thereof -- So be it that I am not of a mind to give unto them of Mine Cup. So be it they shall learn well their lesson --

Now while I have spoken of Peace - let it be said that they shall seek peace within the realm of men - wherein there is No peace -- And when they come unto the Council table with their hearts filled with Love for their fellow men - then We of the Mighty Council shall give unto them the necessary Assistance -- So be it that they but make a Mockery of the "Peace Pacts" - They have No Peace within them -- and they are prone to hatred and greed -- I say: They are prone to hatred and greed - So be it they are given unto bigotry -- When they have given of themself that there be Peace - Then they shall Know the Meaning of Peace -- I say - "Let them Know the Meaning of Peace" - and it shall not be taken from them -- For it shall be established Within them -- So be it I speak for the Good of All -- Let them which have ears hear that which I say. None other shall hear for I say they have put their fingers in their ears that they might Not hear. Let them be. Give unto them No heed Yet ye shall hear Me, and Know that which I say.

So be it I Come that ye might

KNOW even AS I

I AM The Lord thy God

Sananda

> **Recorded by Sister Thedra of the Emerald Cross**

Increase Thine Capacity for Knowledge

Wherein is it said that I shall direct thee? Is it not So? I tell thee for a surety I shall give unto thee that which is necessary for thine Part -- I shall direct thee - and I shall give unto thee that which is necessary for the fulfillment of the Plan --

Let it be said that I am not so foolish as to choke thee - for I Know thy needs -- And ye shall be as ones which Are Prepared for Greater Things -- Yet Greater Things -- I say Increase thine Capacity for Knowledge - and by what means? I say by Application of the Law which is given unto thee -- I say These Laws are sufficient unto thine

Salvation -- APPLICATION is the thing - and without application there is No salvation -- Without Action there is no progress -and without progress there is no Light -- I say - "Let There Be Light" - and there IS Light -- Yet I say - ye shall prepare thyself for to receive it --

And for this have I said I shall direct thee and lead thee - and it is So - For I AM the Light and the Way - So be it that I shall bring thee out of darkness when thou hast so prepared thine self - when thou hast fulfilled thine Covenant -- For I am come that I might fulfill Mine Covenant with thee -- While I say I Am Come to fulfill Mine - I say I have Covenanted with Mine Father - and I am not of a mind to betray Mine Self -- For this have I said I shall find Mine Own then I shall return unto Mine Father which hast sent Me -- Let it be So with thee --

I Am Come that it Be So -- While I say I Am Come that it be So be it As ye Will it --

I AM Sananda

Recorded By Sister Thedra of the Emerald Cross

They Shall Cry for Food Instead of Blood

Wherein is it said that there shall be Great Stress upon the people -- I say Great Stress shall be upon the people - And they shall Cry for Mercy -- While they have given little thought unto the Source of their Being - they shall now ask that they die that it might be ended ---

Yet I say unto them - There is no place wherein thou might escape. For it is given unto Me to Know – For, know ye this - thou shall learn

WELL thine lesson - and for this art thou here within the Earth - as ones under the law of flesh -- When it is said that ye shall learn well thy lesson - It behooves thee to begin to Stir thine self - See that which Goes On about thee - and give unto Me Credit for Knowing - For I See as thou canst Not see -- When thou art free from the law of Earth - Then thou shall See and Know - As I Know - For this do ye wait ---

When it is come that they lay down their Arms - their implements of death - And search for Crumbs - And when they cry out for <u>food instead of blood</u> - Then they shall be as ones prepared to receive Me and that which I have kept for them ---

I say that the ones in high places shall be brought low -- And they too shall remember the day of their feasts - and wonton -- And they too shall cry out ---

While it is given unto Me to see them hold in subjection the poor - sick - and depressed - which cry for bread - I say they too shall want - even as the lowly and the oppressed -- Too I say that they shall bring their children into the market places - to find the Crumbs - which is the refuse from the stalls ---

I say the proud and the haughty shall fall - and the lowly, just - and humble shall be exalted -- Wherein is it said that Justice shall reign Supreme? -- That they shall learn well their lessons? ---

So be it - I do Not Condemn - Neither do I Judge - I Know the Law and I Am Come that they might Know - that they might be as ones Prepared for the Greater Part ---

So be it that I speak unto thee that they might Know that which I Say - for they are deaf unto Mine Words - and they See Not the handwriting on the wall -- So be it I have Written And I Shall Write - and they shall Read that which I shall Write - For it shall be engraven upon their hearts - And they shall Not Forget -- For this is the Time of Remembrance -- So let it Be -- I AM Sananda

Recorded by Sister Thedra of the Emerald Cross

Freedom

Beloved Ones: - When it is given unto thee to be Unbound there shall be no obstruction - no boundaries - no parallels - no place wherein ye can not go - for I say unto thee there is no limitation in Light -- When it is given unto thee to be unbound - and free from the law of gravitation and the attraction of the Moon - ye shall Know that there is Freedom and there is Light! And ye shall See the Light --

While thine eye is blinded at this time it is given unto thee to see in part - which is but a fragment - but a small part of the Whole Plan.

I speak of the Plan -- Yet thou dost Not comprehend the fullness of it - for thou seest in part - wherein there is limitation -- Yet the parts shall be revealed as a Whole --

Now ye shall be as ones which have thine hand in Mine and I shall lead thee - I shall direct thee! I shall give unto thee strength and Power to do that which I have for thee to do --

And it shall become thee to do it with the Grace and Joy of the Initiate. While it is not yet said that ye have Attained - it is said that ye shall walk as One which has Mine Hand upon thee --

So be it that I AM the Lord thy God -

Sananda

Recorded by Sister Thedra of the Emerald Cross

None Innocent

By Mine Hand shall ye be led - And by the Word shall ye be blest - At no time shall I forsake thee - Yet it is given unto thee to See the way in which the dragon moves - It is not clear unto thee that which We of the Realms of Light DO - For We are Not prone to forget the will of the Father which hast sent Us - And His Will is <u>First</u> and <u>Last</u> With Us -- So be it that We are in no hurry - We move as One Body - as One Man for We are in Agreement - We are Not Divided against Ourself - While the ones which serve the dragon divide themself and beguile each other and themself - Wherein have they been united as a whole - as One Body, as Brothers which serve the Light - Which I AM --

I say it is the way of the dragon to divide and destroy that which has been brought forth in the Earth as the Light Manifestation -- I say he has not the mind or the will to Serve the Light - Neither to deliver up his prey - He is the Unscrupulous One - He has the will to hold bound his Subjects -and he shall be as one which has his hand out - he shall snatch from the very cradle of humanity the infant which has come into embodiment for this day that he might gain Great Knowledge - and do a Work Unlike that of the dragon - yet he has forgotten his Mission and he has not the Will to Resist the hand which reaches out to Snatch him -- While it is said that the Ones which come into manifestation in flesh - are innocent Children - be ye not deceived - for they are not innocent in the way of the world! - they have been <u>Well</u> Schooled. While they remember it not - they are nevertheless Schooled - And they shall remember - when it is necessary that they be caused to remember.-

Now ye shall say unto them in Mine Name that there is No Mystery, Only their Unknowing - Nothing Hidden from the Eternal Being which Is - And Always shall Be -- So be it that that Which Is - and shall Always Be - Cannot Forget - and cannot pass away -- So shall it be revealed unto All which Seek the Light - Which I AM --

I Am Sent that there be Comprehension

Within the Realm of Man - I bid them

Arise - Come Up Higher - And Abide in the Light. I AM that I AM

Sananda

Recorded by Sister Thedra of the Emerald Cross

The Ever Present I am

Behold in Me the Light Which I AM - and Know ye that I Am Come that ye might have Light more abundantly -- Seek ye First the Light - and I shall reveal Mineself unto thee -- Know ye that there is none Other Way into the Father's House save through Me - for I Am the Door -- I AM the door through which ye enter in -- While it is written I Am the Truth, the Way - I Am the Door -- for none come save through Me --It is given unto ME to be the "Gate Keeper" and none pass save they Are

Prepared -- It is said: "None pass save through Me" - for I AM the Light that lighteth every Man which Comes into the realm of flesh - Such is "The Way" -- And it behooves thee to make ready thineself for to enter into the Realm of Light - wherein I abide -- So be it that I Am the Lord thy God - Sent of Mine Father that there be Light -- So let it Be -- Let it Be! - - Let It BE --

For in the world of darkness there is need for Light -- Yet I Am there - I Am not limited -- I say - Seek ye the Light - And I shall reveal Mine Self - for I go not - I come not -- I AM --

I AM the Lord thy God

Sananda

Recorded by Sister Thedra of the Emerald Cross

One Harmonious Whole
All Fragments Fit Together

Beloved Ones - It is given unto Me to be One of the Host -- And I Am Come that ye might be given the Assistance necessary unto thine learning -- As each one has a part - and no two parts are alike -- Yet All parts blend in One Harmonious Whole -- where there is beauty and Symmetry - I say there are no rough and ugly edges within the Whole for All Fragments and small parts shall fit together as One Beauteous Whole when the Plan is finished -- There shall be light and dark - there shall be Golds and Blues of many hues and Not One Piece shall be out of place - or in any way misplaced -- These shall be as the "Whole" and not one part or piece shall be discounted --

Ye shall remember Well - the trials and the heartaches - that ye might be of Greater Service unto thine fellow man -- Ye shall give unto him as ye have received - and ye shall neither condemn - nor be unto him the Judge - for no man can judge his Brother --

I say be ye not judged by his standards -- For thou shall walk as one Alone -- Wherein is it said that ye shall Stand Steadfast and ask of no man his opinion - his blessing -- Ye shall Know upon what Foundation thou hast builded - and it shall not fail -- It shall prevail - And this Altar Shall Endure for I See and Know - for I Am One which has the Greater Vision -- I Know -- And I Am Not Deceived -- So be it I Am One which is Sent that ye might be comforted --

So let it be I Am the One which shall be Known Simply as Sananda

Recorded by Sister Thedra of the Emerald Cross

No Small Parts

Behold the New Day and rejoice that it is Come - For Mighty shall be the Light thereof -- I say unto thee the Light shall flood the Earth and it shall bring about New and Powerful Manifestations - And at no time hast thine eyes beheld such as ye shall see -- For the Greatest of thine accomplishments shall be as nought in comparison --

I tell thee of a surety thine work is not finished - for there is yet work to do which ye know not of -- And at no time shall ye deny that which is offered unto thee in Mine Name - for it is given unto Me to give unto thee the part which is necessary at this time - And at no time is it to be discounted or taken as trivial - for there are No Trivial Parts in Mine House - or within the Plan -- I say - the Plan has many Parts and at no time are ye to discount thine or call it trivial -- I say It is for the Small Parts that the plan is fulfilled ---

So be it I have Spoken and thou hast heard Me --

I AM Sananda

The Fullness of His Glory

Berean

Behold this day the New - The Glorious <u>New</u> - For the <u>Old</u> shall pass and be no more - And the <u>New</u> shall be the Glory of which thou hast not yet dreamed - for I say unto thee - thine eyes hast not beheld the Glory which is to be -- Ye shall behold the Hand Work of the Lord - and ye shall call It Good. It shall be Good - and ye shall See it for that which it Is --

Ye shall be glad that the Old hast passed and the <u>New</u> is made Manifest -- While I say unto thee - thine eyes hast Not Yet beheld the Glory of the Lord thy God - I say ye shall!

And ye shall Know that which ye See -- While it is given unto thee to be in the world of men as ones bound in flesh - ye can not image the fullness of His Glory!

When it is Come that ye stand Face to Face with Him - Ye shall Know that which I Say unto thee - and ye shall be Glad that ye have been prepared -- So let it Be --

For this have I Spoken unto thee that ye might be blest --

So be it I Am

Berean -

Recorded by Sister Thedra of the Emerald Cross

The Word Which Goes Out from the Council

Beloved of Mine Being -- Be ye blest this day - and give unto them this Word -- And for this is it given unto thee - that they might Know that which I say -- For their ears are sealed and they know not that which I say unto them -- Now let them which have ears to hear - hear that which I say -- And them which have their fingers in their ears - remove them that they hear -- The ones which have a Will to hear shall be made to hear -- So be it that I Am Come that they might Know that which I say. While it is given unto Me to be One of the Host I say it is Mine Part to Assist the Plan - the bringing forth - the fulfilling of the Plan --

So be it that even the "WORD" which goes out from the Council in this manner is of Sacred Account -- and not to be discounted - for it brings with it a blessing and a Vibration - which shall bless All which doth Will to be brought Out of bondage -- And it is Mine Part to Add Mine Part - for without it the Plan would not be perfect or Complete -- It is part of their preparation that they Accept All Parts which is Given unto them -- And yet there shall be so many parts that they Could Not Read Recite - or Remember or purchase with their present means of exchange. Therefore it is by means of the <u>Mighty</u> <u>Power</u> of the Word which goes out upon the <u>eth</u> that they find themself enabled to reach up higher to Communicate with the Mighty Council - and with the Father-Mother-God --

Now I say: - When they do reject the "Word" they reject the One which sends it forth -- They seal their ears with their own fingers - for none other is responsible for their deafness.

Let it be understood that there are None so sad as the ones which think themself wise! None so sad as the ones which betray himself -- and these <u>Are</u> the traitors -- Now when it is come that they have come to Know where from they Came - and Whither they goest - I say - they might call themself "WISE" - Yet not before!

For they are in darkness - and Know Not that they are bound!

When it is Come that they are free from the gravitation of the Earth and the Attraction of the Moon <u>then</u> they shall be free from the law of flesh - and that which holds them bound.

Yet they shall endure unto the end - when they shall be so prepared that they Step Forth from the dense body of flesh into their body of Light Substance which is <u>Not</u> of Earth -- And then they shall be free of their bounds -- Yet they shall be as ones prepared - through and <u>by</u> the "WORD" which shall go out from the mouth of the Great and Mighty One - which We Know as the "Host of Hosts" Which is called the Great Grand Master --

Now when it is Come that they might be freed from the bonds of flesh - they shall receive As they are prepared - As they have prepared themself to receive - So be it that they shall receive as they are prepared, Each put into his proper place – environment. And none shall be alone for he shall find his own kind. When he has prepared himself to receive the King - the King shall show Himself -- When he has <u>served well</u> the Dragon - the "Dragon" shall be there to swallow him up - to devour him to hold him bound - and he shall cry for deliverance -- Such is the way of the traitor which serves the forces of darkness - which has taken the form of the "Black Dragon" --

So be it I Come that I might add Mine blessing - that there be Greater Light -- So let it be for the Light shall not be hidden -- While they might hold their hands before their face that they See it Not - they shall have the power and the will to remove them - for none other shall do it for them -- They are their own porter - So be it I have Spoken and thou hast heard Me - and ye shall be blest of Me and by Me -- I AM Berean

For This---

Behold in Me the Light Which I Am - and Know ye that I AM the Lord thy God --

I say <u>Behold</u> the Hand Move - See it move - and Know ye that it moveth Swiftly and with Perfection -- For there is No darkness within the Light which I Am -- And at No time shall I be found Wanting -- So be it that I Am the One Sent of Mine Father - that His Kingdom be set up - and for this have I given of Mineself -- So be it that I have set forth the Law which shall govern the Work which shall go into the building of His Kingdom --

And it is for this that I say unto thee: "Be ye as ones prepared for that which shall be given unto thee to do". And it shall be for this preparation that ye shall be as Ones Acceptable unto the Mighty Council - Unto the Plan -- For this have I Spoken that ye be Prepared.

So Let It Be -- I AM Sananda

Recorded by Sister Thedra of the Emerald Cross

The Glory of the Heavens

Beloved Ones: - When it is Come that thine work is finished and thine time is come that ye be lifted up - ye shall be given a New body of Light Substance - and that body shall be no part of the Earth substance - for it shall be made of the Source of All the Earth Substance - from out which cometh All other Substance - And it shall be Pure in Substance, Uncontaminated by manifestation of any kind --

While I say it shall be uncontaminated by manifestation - I say that it shall be uncontaminated by man's conditions which is of a lower substance -- Wherein hast thou Seen the Contamination? Wherein hast thou Seen the Pure Substance of the Uncontaminated Light from which thine New Body shall be made? I tell thee of a Surety thou hast Not seen Such Glory! So be it that the Glory of the Heavens shall be Opened up - and ye shall See and Know that it is for thine Own Sake that We the Mighty Host hast Stood By that ye might be prepared to See and Know -- So be it that I Am One of the Host -- So be it I bless thee with Mine Presence -

I AM

Recorded by Sister Thedra of the Emerald Cross

Behold Me

Behold in Me the Light Which I AM -- I AM The Light - I AM The Life - I AM The Way - and I AM the ALL - The Pure Substance from Which All Things Come --- I AM the Alpha and the Omega - The First and the Last --

I AM the Un Manifest

I AM the Manifested

I the Word

I AM the Action

I AM the Result of the Word

I AM the First and the Last of All that was or ever shall Be

I AM the Sum Total of All that thou shall become - for in the beginning I Was and thou wast with Me as Mine Own Self -- And for this wast thou Mine Own Being -- And wherein hast thou been one separated from Me? --

Wherein hast thou been separate - and apart from Me? -- I say unto thee - thou Art Not Separate from Me except within thine <u>thinking</u> -- Think ye Not thou art a thing apart -- For n'ere was it so - for from Me thou couldst Not BE ---

So be it I AM thine Parent Eternal

Recorded by Sister Thedra of the Emerald Cross

It is Come When the Son of Man Shall Come into His Own

Sanat Kumara

Sanat Kumara Speaking - Beloved of Mine Being - Give unto them these Mine Words and say unto them in Mine Name that the day is come when the Son of Man shall Come into His Own - When He shall arise and be as One - when he shall become the Sons of God - When he shall come into his rightful estate and walk upright as Children of God.

He shall come to Know that he is not Chemical man - that he is more, That he has an Inheritance which has been Kept for him - when he has given himself up completely unto the "Will of Our Father" - Then he shall be as a Son of God - for he has then become a fit Vessel that he might Glorify the Father --

I say that when he hast Given of himself Completely and Irrevocably unto the Will of Our Father (the Cause of his Being) then he shall be as a fit Vessel - that he might receive his inheritance -- And until he has rid himself of his 'puny way' - his resentments - his fortune which he hast begotten of men - his little notions - preconceived ideas and All of his idolatry - he is in No way prepared to receive his Inheritance in full - for he is filled with his own darkness and guile -- He has not the mind which can Comprehend the Light - for darkness is within him --

So be it that I am Come that there be Light in the world of men -- I come that My Light be added unto Mine Brothers' which have labored long and tirelessly for their deliverance -- While it is given unto Us to be of the Host - I say thou too - art part of the "Noble Assembly" -- So be it I appoint thee Mine Spokesman that they might have this Mine

Word unto them -- So be it and Selah -- I am not finished Mine Word - Yet I shall bid thee Go and feed the hungry flock which await the "Word". So let them which doth hunger be fed and satisfied.

Sanat Kumara

Sanat Kumara

Blessed One:

Would You explain to us - (them) the difference between the "Sons of Men" and the "Sons of God"? - Thedra

"The Sons of God are the Ones which have been lifted up, out of their bondage and out of their filthy condition which they as the Sons of Men have created for themself"

What of the Chemical man - This expression shall be new to some which "read" this Word?

"By the fortune of being born of woman - they have blanked from them their memory of All that is Real and Eternal -

Their entire condition becomes one of surrounding darkness - dense matter - and they are influenced by their surroundings forgetting that they have Not been of man and woman created -- Yet they take upon themself bodies of chemical nature - which they wear for a time as a garment which is tossed aside as such -- And these things they Know Not! -- These things they <u>KNOW</u> <u>NOT</u>! - for they remember them Not. Now when it is said they are as "Chemical Men" I say they walk as robots as Soulless ones - Knowing not their Source - Motivated by the thoughts of "Mass Mind" "Others thinking" the opinions of other men which they have compiled through their blindness and stumblings -- That which they have seen as through lenses conditioned by their own experience --

Now I say unto them - When it is come that one gives himself over to the thinking of another he hast sold his inheritance for a poor pottage. So be it I shall speak again on this subject -- Have I not said it before?

So shall I say it again!

I Am Come that there be Light - So Be It --

I AM

Thine Older Brother

Sanat Kumara

Recorded by Sister Thedra of the Emerald Cross

The False - The True
The Spinner of the Web

Sori Sori - Beloved of Mine Being. Have I not said that I would speak again on the subject of the "Sons of Man" -- And for this do I speak unto thee now --

Let it be said that the time is come when they shall come to Know the True from the False -- The false shall pass as No thing - and be remembered no more -- While the True/Real - shall be known and remembered -- Yet it is now come when the false shall be exposed for that which he is - and he shall be as the one which shall expose himself! When he exposes himself unto the Light - he can not bear it - for he is false - And so long as he serves the forces of darkness he shall be tormented -- And he shall attempt to hide his falsehood behind a respectable name - A respectable front as it were -- A "wolf in sheep's clothing" thou wouldst understand --

While he weaves/spins many webs for others - he but traps himself therein -- And at no time shall ye put thine foot into his web -- At no time shall ye be Caught off Guard - for I have spoken unto thee in riddles/parables - that ye might Comprehend that which I say -- So be it that I am Come that ye be prepared for the Greater Part --

So be it - I shall lead thee -

I AM Sananda

Recorded by Sister Thedra of the Emerald Cross

The Eternal Parent Speaks: "Because of Me"

Behold in Me the Light Which I AM - for I AM the Light Which lights every man which Is or ever shall Be - For his Being Is of Me and because of Me - which Was and ever shall Be - For I AM the Light - I AM the Truth - I AM the Life - and from Me there is naught which shall endure --

I say unto thee - should the Light not exist there would be no shadows - and thou art within the shadows -- Therefore thou Seeth as faintly - thou hast not Comprehended the fullness of the Light Which I AM -- I Am Come that ye Might Comprehend -- Yet I say unto thee - the shadows shall not endure when the fullness of the Light is Comprehended - for within the fullness of the Light there <u>is</u> no darkness. While thou art as ones now walking in bondage - therein is the darkness which shall pass as <u>nothing</u> -- And it shall be remembered No more --

And for this have I sent unto thee Mine Sons that ye might be brought out of bondage -- When it is given unto thee to be unbound ye shall rejoice that the shadows have passed into the unreality and remembered no more - for they shall not exist! They shall be as no thing which shall be eternally without reality - for ye shall give the fortunes of darkness no power over thee, for it is given unto every man which is unbound to return unto his rightful place, the place from which he went out -- And therein he shall find that he is At Home -- He is no Stranger That many await his coming - That he has been <u>as</u> <u>one</u> <u>asleep</u> and he shall <u>well</u> remember them which awaits him --

He shall be as a Son long away - which hast returned triumphantly VICTORIOUS! And he shall be glad for his Awakening -- Let Us rejoice for his Awakening shall be Cause for rejoicing.

So be it I have Spoken from out the Source of Light - and thou hast heard that which I have said unto thee -- For this have I given unto thee Gift of Hearing - So let it profit them which are of a mind to receive it.

For it is for the Ones which are of like mind --

I AM that I AM

I AM thine Parent Eternal

Solen Aum Solen

Recorded by Sister Thedra of the Emerald Cross

The Greatest Generation First Born

Beloved Ones - While it is Mine Part to be the Lord of Lords the Host of Hosts - it is thine part to be One of the Host -- And it is given unto thee to be part of the Noble Company - For thou Art of the First Born,- which is the Greatest Generation - It is the Generation to which I belong.

For I Am of the First Born - which makes of Me the "Royal Son" and I Know Mine Lineage -- I have not forgotten Mine lineage as thou hast. While thou hast not remembered it for a time - I say ye shall come to Know that which thou hast forgotten ---

When it is come that ye are so prepared that I shall touch thee - and ye have been so prepared for to receive thine Memory ye shall be Glad for it is given unto ME to Know thine Inheritance -- And it is Mine Part to restore thine memory - when it is come that ye are prepared to receive it.

None shall pilfer thine inheritance or take it from thee -- Thou hast but forfeited it for a time -- Now ye shall be as ones prepared to receive it ---

When I say - "Be ye as ones prepared" - I say it is the Way of the Dragon to beguile thee - and to give unto thee that which would deter thee and turn thee aside -- And it is for this that I remind thee of thine part -- I say unto thee - Keep thine own council - and let no man turn thee aside -- While it is given unto many to speak of Me and to speak the Words which are accredited unto Mine saying - I tell thee of a surety that I Am in no way the puny priest they make of Me -- I AM NOT Limited by their concept of Me - or about Me.

When they speak of Me as He which <u>was</u> called such and such - they are not aware of Me as I AM - as the One Which IS - and Always shall BE --

I AM neither limited by <u>time</u> - <u>space</u> - or law of any kind - for I AM ONE with Mine Father -- I AM His Hand and His Feet made manifest.- I AM that I AM --- I Am <u>Not</u> limited by form - I can and <u>do</u> take any form suitable for Mine purpose - for I AM the Master of the Elements out of which I Will the forms I use for <u>Mine</u> <u>Purpose</u> ---

While it is given unto me to have the POWER and Authority to do these things - I do not perform magic that <u>they</u> be satisfied -- I Am Not an entertainer - I Am Come that there be <u>Light</u>! - that they be free from their bondage - Yet it is said they shall free themself of All their preconceived ideas of and about ME - for I Am the sum total of that which they shall BECOME -- So be it I shall speak again this day -- Let it Be --

I AM the Lord thy God

Sananda

Recorded by Sister Thedra of the Emerald Cross

Ponder Well these Mine Sayings Sananda

Sananda Speaking unto the traitors - He Sayeth:

Behold that which thou hast fortuned unto thineself! Behold that which thou hast done! - See the way in which thou hast served the DRAGON - See the results thereof -- And Know ye that therein is thine downfall -- I say unto thee: The Lord thy God - hast made it possible for thee to be as the pore - in which the Spirit of man dwelleth - The Spirit which animates the "pore" is the indwelling "Christ" and wherein have ye betrayed thine Self? - I say unto thee: Look no further for the Anti-Christs - Thou art the ANTICHRISTS for thou hast betrayed thineself!

Thou hast looked afar - and pointed thine <u>unholy</u> finger at thine brother and said: "Behold that Pagan, See his <u>sins</u> and be unto him his <u>Advisor</u> - make of him a man after mine own image - after "our" image fashion him into a robot like unto us -- for he is as nothing until he is made in "Our" image and likeness"!

Now I say unto them which have <u>set themself up</u> - as paragons of Christ-ianity - that they are Not the Christians which they <u>think</u> themself to be -- for they have betrayed the Holy-Cause!!

I Am Not deceived by their honeyed word -- They have not hidden their nefarious schemes from Me -- For Light which I AM - comprehends the darkness - Yet the darkness comprehends not the Light!! ---

I say unto them which deny Mine Words: Thou Art of the "Anti-Christ" - for I Am Come - declaring the TRUTH - yet ye have not the mind to comprehend the <u>Truth</u> - neither do ye Know ME - For thou art bound by the dragon -- Ye serve him diligently /faithfully and constantly -- Ye know not the power which he holds over thee - for thou hast been <u>his</u> faithful slave -- Ye have given thine self over unto his dictates - his power hast held thee bondage - for I say - thou art enslaved --

Wherein hast thou denied him or his hold upon thee - Wherein hast thou attempted to overthrow him? Wherein hast thou denied him his due? --

Wherein hast thou given unto him credit for his part in thine own tribulation -- Wherein hast thou set him up as the "Great and Mighty" and bowed down before him? --

I say unto them: Ye have made IDOLS of thine own imaging and worshiped them -- Now ye shall be scattered knowing not from whence cometh thine confusion -- Yet ye shall be confused - and scattered - Knowing not which way to turn -- I speak unto them which serve the forces of darkness --

I speak that they might Know from whence cometh their suffering Wherein they are held in bondage/darkness - knowing not by which they are bound ---

Now I speak unto them which Serve the Light which I AM: Therein is thine Salvation - Therein is the Light from which cometh <u>thine</u> direction - thine help - thine strength - and from which cometh thine <u>help</u> -- Be ye not deceived by the ones which cryeth "Fools!" - for I say they Know Not they are the servants of the <u>Dark</u> <u>One</u> -- the "Son of Perdition".

Let them be - let them be - for they shall bring about their own downfall -- <u>Keep</u> <u>thine</u> <u>eye</u> <u>single</u> -- And See that which ye do -- And be ye as one Spotless! --

<u>Keep</u> <u>thine</u> <u>hands</u> Clean and serve the Light with All thine heart - mind - and BEING -- Feign not wisdom - Ponder Well these Mine sayings -- And be ye blest --

For I AM COME that ye be blest - So Let It Be -

I AM Sanannda

Recorded by Sister Thedra of the Emerald Cross

The Spirit Sayeth Come and be Free

Beloved Ones - Mine hand I place upon thee and I pronounce the Word: "Let there be Understanding" -- And so shall there Be -- For I Am Come that ye might have comprehension - and ye shall be glad for Mine Hand, For without It thou should walk in darkness -- I say unto thee - I Come that there be Light -- So be it that I AM the Lord thy God - and at no time have I given unto thee the bitter dregs ---

So be it that I AM not of a mind to forsake thee nor leave thee alone I tell thee of a Surety that I Am Come that Mine Covenant with thee be fulfilled "this day" -- Now let it be understood that the / is without limitation and it is for this that I have said "All the Father has is Thine" for it Is So! - And it is given unto thee to be limited in Flesh -- Flesh is perishable -- While that which is Eternal perishes Not -- I say "That which is <u>ETERNAL</u> perishes Not!"

Now while it is given unto material form to pass as the shadows before the noonday Sun - it is the Way of the Eternal Spirit to be forever Free and Unbound -- It is the eyes of flesh which doth behold limitation. Yet the Spirit Sayeth Come - And it is given unto Me to See the flesh give way unto the call of the Spirit -- I say the Spirit Sayeth Come! and be ye free forevermore -- So be it that I Am Come that there be Light - For this have I lain Mine Hand upon thee --

I bid thee give unto Me Credence for Knowing that which I say unto thee --

So Be It -

I AM

Sananda

Recorded by Sister Thedra of the Emerald Cross

To Know is Wisdom

Sanat Kumara Speaking - When it is given unto thee to Know the fullness of the Light - Ye shall be as One Liberated from All darkness and bondage -- The Light is the Light - and it is No part of darkness -- And for this do I say unto thee: "To Know is Wisdom" - For none can speak of the Light Knowingly until he is liberated -- And so long as he walks in darkness he Knows Not the fullness of the Light - he hast but a <u>Glimmer</u> -- And this conditions his life - his actions - his <u>thinking</u> --

Now I say unto thee: "To Know is Wisdom" - To Know is to BE - and to BE is to Know -- Wherein is it said: "Preparation is thine Becoming?" Ye Become that which ye prepare thineself to BEcome --

Wherein is it said: "Be ye as one filled with Love - filled with Joy. Be ye at Peace" - Such is Mine Word unto thee -- Since when have they loved One Another? And for the second time I ask thee - Wherein is it said: Be ye at Peace - and be ye filled with Joy? -- I am Come that it Be. And for this have I given of Mineself that it be So -- I say - I have given of MINESELF that they might "Know" - For to <u>think</u> is the results of their uncertainty -- their insanity - Yea I say: "Their insanity" For they have thought themself Wise - when they stand on the brink of destruction -- And have We of the Mighty Host not spoken of this many times? Yet they plunge headlong into the fire - Knowing not that it BURNS! Poor heedless fools! --

I say - they "Think" themself Wise! - It is said: "Father forgive them they Know Not that which they do" - Yet I tell thee of a Surety - the LAW is Exacting - and it plays No favorites - It is impartial and Knows No bounds - It is the exact equation of All the Law - and Nothing - No man shall invalidate it -- There are None Exempt! --

I have spoken that they might Know the Consequence of their wanton --

So be it - I shall speak again -

I AM thine Older Brother -

Sanat Kumara

Recorded by Sister Thedra of the Emerald Cross

Spirit Heareth What the Spirit Sayeth

Son of God am I -- Son of God art thou -- Behold in Me the fulfillment of the Law -- <u>Behold</u> in Me the fulfillment of the Covenant -- For when the Covenant is fulfilled with Me - Ye shall Be As I AM - For then thou shall Know thine Self as I Know thee --

So let it Be As the Father hast Willed it - and at no time shall ye be cast out --

Be ye as One which has Mine Hand upon thee - and I shall lead thee into the Place wherein I AM -- For this do I speak unto thee -- Let it be said that thine hands shall be Mine hands, thine feet Mine feet -and they shall be Swift to do Mine Work. For are We not One? -- I say unto <u>thee</u>: We Are One -- Know ye this and divide Not thine Self from Me. Draw Not away, For I AM and thou Art As Mine Self made flesh. So be it I AM Not a <u>thing</u> Apart from thee - For thou Art Not flesh - <u>Thou Art Spirit</u> - Spirit Divine -- And for this have I Spoken unto thee - for <u>Spirit heareth what the Spirit Sayeth</u> -- So be it I have Great things in store for thee -- I AM that I AM -- So be it - I AM

Sananda

Recorded by Sister Thedra of the Emerald Cross

The Celestial Music
None Shall be Deprived of Its Echo

Sori Sori - Sweet is the Word - And it shall ring out clear and Sweet -- None shall be deprived of its echo -- None shall be deprived of its

Music - for it shall peal out as the thunder - it shall be loud and Clear! I say they shall fall upon their face and cry - For the sheer Joy of the Musical Notes shall move them unto the depth of their Being - and they shall See that which no eyes before hast ever beheld! For I say unto thee there shall be such Glorious Manifestation which shall be as none hast imaged -- For all thine poets and Artists have not as yet captured such Beauty and Grandeur --

While I say it is Not given unto mortal eyes to have Seen such Glories - they shall -- Yet they shall turn their face away - for the blinding Light shall be more than they can bear -- Let it be - for these have not Known such beauty - and they shall be afrightened to look upon it -- Their eyes shall be accustomed unto the darkness of their accustomed habitats - and they shall wonder why they are so privileged to behold such sights -- Yet I say unto thee Behold the Glory of the Lord -- For I am Come that ye might be so prepared --

So be it - I AM He-

Sananda

Recorded by Sister Thedra of the Emerald Cross

Let Him Which is Without Sin Cast the First Stone

Beloved of Mine Being -- Give unto them these Mine Words and be ye blest -- For I say unto thee thou art Mine Hand made flesh and for this I say - "Give unto them these Mine Words" -- When it is given unto them to be prepared for to receive Mine Word then I shall speak unto them -- Yet they are as ones unprepared - So be it I come that they might be prepared - Let it be so -- For this do I manifest Mineself in flesh --

Wherein is it said that - "they shall come into the age of accountability"? So shall it be - Yet they are now as ones playing with 'dangerous things' -- They Know not the results of their experiments - Their ways are not of Me - - Their way leads unto bitterness and degradation -- While they shall cry out for surcease from the results of all their experiments - they shall learn well their bitter lesson -- While it is given unto Me to be the Mother Eternal - I shall not deprive them their own free will - neither their lessons though bitter they be!

Wherein is it said that - "They shall grow into the age of accountability and be as ones responsible for themself"?

Now it is come when they shall choose which way -- They shall choose for themself - for no man shall take from them their free will -- While it is given unto man to be the Keeper of the laws - set forth that they might Keep the law and walk in the way set before them -- It is given unto the irresponsible to be the ones which beset the Keepers of the law -- These are the wayward ones which shall learn that they can not misuse the energy allotted them without bitter results -- Wherein is it said: "None Escape the Law"? It is So -- So be it that None escape!

When these rebellious ones have learned well their lessons they shall be as ones prepared for the Greater part --

Be ye not troubled for them for they are not alone - be it the hard way they have chosen -- They shall learn the hard way -- While it is a long and hard way - they shall remember their suffering and torment.

Now while it is given unto others to seek the Light - I say these shall be as ones prepared to receive it - and they shall no more remember their suffering and torment for they shall be as nothing - be no more- for the illusion shall pass from them --

Wherein is it said that "The Way of The Transgressor is hard"? So be it True!

I have reminded them of their transgressions and responsibility - yet they go headlong into the fortunes of darkness - They enmesh themself within the web which the Son of perdition has spun for them.- I say pity them Not! Lest ye become part of their plight -- So be it I have spoken of this and thou hast heard Me --

I am Come that there be Peace within thine heart -- Let not thine heart be troubled - for long have I awaited thine return -- Long have I watched thine suffering and sorrow -- So be it Mine Love is Greater than thine - for thou hast not remembered My Great Love and Compassion for thee -- I have watched thine going and coming with Great Love and Compassion - yet I have not deprived thee thine lessons. So be it I await thine return ---

I AM thine Mother Eternal

Recorded by Sister Thedra

Let Them Eat of Mine Bread

By Mine Own Hand I shall lead thee -- I shall direct thee and portion out that which is necessary unto thee for the Good of the Plan -- It is

Mine Part to give unto thee that which is for the Good of All -- And for this do I Give unto thee the Word which is meant for them -- When it is Come that they have no need for it - I shall give unto them No More.- And I say them which think themself Self-sufficient shall find that they have Not Known their weakness - for their weakness shall trip them up. Yet I say that they shall learn that they live not alone - neither do they live by bread alone -- While they labor for bread - it is given unto them to pay the price - And when they ask of <u>thee</u> for <u>bread</u> thou givest freely.

I say that it is given freely - while they pay the price for that which fills their bellies --

So be it that they Know Not the Worth of the Bread which I have for them -- Let them eat thereof and hunger no more.

So be it and Selah --

For this have I portioned it out --

I AM Sananda

Recorded by Sister Thedra of the Emerald Cross

The Old Law -- New Dispensation

Blest of Me Art Thou - for I Am Come that ye be blest -- While I give of Mineself that ye be blest - thou givest unto others that they be blest,- So be it that they Know Not the fullness of that which I AM -- Yet they shall come into the Knowledge of Me and Know that I Am - and that they walk Not alone -- So be it that I Am the Lord thy God - and it is given unto Me to be the Director of this New Dispensation - They which are of a mind to follow Me shall come into the New Day with the Light which I AM --

And they shall be given that which hast been held in trust for them for This Day I say unto them - they shall no longer come under the 'Old Law' - they shall no longer be bound by the 'Old Law' - they shall be given a New Law - A New Dispensation whereby they might be unbound <u>this</u> day - And they shall be as ones prepared for to be so unbound -- They shall be glad it is come when they shall Know Me as I AM --

Now while it is said that "They shall no longer come under the Old Law" I say - they shall obey the law set down before them -- Yet they shall be as ones which have fulfilled that law - the old - and come into Greater revelation - into the Light -- For I say the law is given unto them which hast need of it -- When it is given unto them to have fulfilled All the law - then they No longer have need of it -- Thus sayeth the Lord of Hosts --

So be it that I Am Come that the law be fulfilled with them For I have covenanted with Mine people and I Am Not a traitor -- So be it I speak unto thee that <u>they</u> might Know <u>Me</u> and about Me -- For they as a whole have made a mockery of Me - of Mine Work - Mine Words -- They have made an <u>Idol</u> of Me - And they have fortuned unto themself much darkness -- They Know Me Not!!

I Am Come that they might have Light

So let them Come which thirsteth

And they shall drink of Mine Cup --

Be it Sweet --

So be it I AM

Sananda

Recorded by Sister Thedra of the Emerald Cross

Thine Thinking Hast Not Made It So

Sori Sori -- Be ye blest this day and give unto them this Mine Word -- And let it be unto them food and drink -- When it is said that there shall be Great manifestation such as they have not seen - it is given unto Me to Know -- For I have seen that which shall come into manifestation - For I am not limited by time or space - neither distance --

I Know no distance for I go not neither do I come -- For I Am <u>there,</u> I Am <u>here</u> - and it becomes Me to be at All times in the place wherein I Am - for I Am the Ever-present Omnipotent Being that I AM --

When it is said - that "I Come" - it is that I Am with thee for the purpose of thine own <u>awareness</u> - that ye might Know that I Am -- And because I Am thou Art -- For there is no separation - no division as We are One -- And because of <u>thine</u> <u>thinking</u> - <u>thou</u> <u>hast</u> <u>thought</u> us as separate - as divided

N'ere was it so - For there is no separation - For thine thinking hast NOT made it So -- Thine thinking hast created thine illusions and all the misery which thou hast experienced. So be it that I tell thee of a surety - thou art One With Me -- For this do I say unto thee thou Art Mine Hands and Mine feet made manifest --

So be it I AM the Lord thy God -

Sananda

Recorded by Sister Thedra of the Emerald Cross

Behold the Light – Then Ye Shall Know Me

Sananda

Beloved Ones -- Wherein is it said that the day begins anew This is a new day - and for that I say unto thee rejoice - lay aside all thine old ways and rejoice that the old is past - and take upon thineself Mine Armor and rejoice -- For I have called thee out from among them and they shall be unto thee that which thou hast left behind -- I say let them be - Follow ye Me - and be as one free from the way of the world -- Seek ye the Light which I Am - Let not thine feet be leaden - Let not thine heart be burdened for them - For I say "Come" let thine feet be swift to do Mine Work - thine tongue swift to speak the Words which I shall put into thine mouth --

It shall be given unto Mine servants to speak Mine Words While they shall Not put words into Mine Mouth -- While the ones which Know not shall poll-parrot Mine sayings - that they might justify <u>their</u> unbelief - their own preconceived ideas and idolatry -- I say: "They shall poll-parrot Mine sayings* to justify their unbelief - and their own opinions – and idolatry -- So be it that I Am Come that they might have

Light – Too, I say - there are none so blind as the ones which <u>will</u> <u>Not</u> <u>See</u> -- I say "Behold In Me the Light Which I AM - and Know ye that I Am the Lord thy God sent that ye be delivered out of bondage -- I say Behold the Light and Know wherein ye are staid -- And then ye shall Know Me - for I AM the Light - the Life - the Way-- See ye the Light and be ye blest -- For this have I revealed Mineself -- So be it I Am Sent of Mine Father that ye be brought out of bondage.

I AM Sananda

Recorded by Sister Thedra of the Emerald Cross

* Quote from "The Bible"

Behold the Glory of the Lord

Beloved Ones - While it is as yet not visible unto thee I say there is a Great and Mighty Host which shall become apparent - which shall be Seen - and it shall be heard -- And ye shall rejoice for thine hearing -- For it shall be as nothing thou hast ever heard -- I say ye shall rejoice that ye have the ears to hear - and ye shall be glad! --

While thine mortal eyes are not Capable of the Sight -- While they are blind unto such Glory - I tell thee thine eyes shall be made to see - thine eye shall be single - and ye shall S<u>ee</u> the Glory of the Lord -- And ye shall Cry Out for Joy -- So be it I Know -- I Am Come that ye might Know -- So be it that I Am the Lord thy God - and I speak Knowing of such Glory - that which thou hast Not Seen with thine mortal eyes – I Say Behold the Glory of the LORD - I AM Sananda

Behold the Glory of God!!!

Sori Sori -- Beloved Ones - which have come unto this Altar: Let it be said that the Way is made Straight - that the door now is Opened wide and for this do We bid thee enter -- I say we bid thee Enter!! Pass ye into the Inner Temple - and be ye as Ones which has been prepared --

I say - "PASS ye into the Inner Temple and be ye as Ones prepared". While it is not yet Known that which ye shall find therein - it doth appear unto thee that it is but a dream - an illusion -- Yet I say there is <u>Nothing</u> in thine world so Real for it is the "REAL" and thine world shall pass away --

I say: "Behold ye the Glory of God!"

Behold ye the Glory of God!

Behold ye the Glory of God!

So let it Be!

I AM Sananda

Recorded by Sister Thedra of the Emerald Cross

Life Versus Illusion

Mine Beloved Children - It is now come when thou shall be aware of Me - and Know from whence thou hast gone forth I say - ye shall come into the awareness of thine Being One with Me - and ye shall remember Me and that which I have endowed unto thee as Mine Children -- So be it that thou hast forgotten -- Let it not trouble thee - for I say unto thee ye shall remember -- So be it I have decreed it So.

Now when it is come that thou hast finished thine sojourn within flesh - ye shall step forth from thine old body of flesh and take unto thineself thine Celestial body which is already for thee -- Thou hast but to claim it -- I say: Ye shall step forth from thine old body of flesh - and be as one which has a body of Light Substance - that which is perfect - that which is without blemish --

Then ye shall be as I have decreed it - for I have not decreed thine illusion - thine dream world -- It is not of Mine Creation - for that which I create is perfect and real - it perishes not --

While I say that which I create takes many - many forms, changes as the colors of the rainbow - yet it it passeth not - for the creation is perfect - and it is created for change - it goes in - and out - of one form into another - creating Great and Powerful rhythm within the Whole -- There is no discordant notes within the Reality of Mine Creation --

So be ye aware of Mine Handiwork - and rejoice that it is Perfect - for it is So -- So let it be --

I AM thine Parent -

Solen Aum Solen

Recorded by Sister Thedra of the Emerald Cross

That Ye Might Come into the Fullness of Thine Stature

Beloved Ones -- It is said and wisely so that there are many called and few are chosen -- I tell thee of a surety that thine calling is certain -- Yet thou hast not attained the <u>fullness</u> of thine inheritance -- It is not yet given unto thee to know the measure of thine Stature ---

I say - thou knowest not the measure of thine Stature -- While it is given unto Me to know -- I see - and I am not deceived -- Be it so that thou ART SONS of GOD - thou hast <u>not</u> received the fullness of thine inheritance -- I Am come that ye might know -- While I stand ready to give unto thee that which I have kept for thee - I say it is not yet come when thou art ready to receive it ---

When thou hast finished that which thou hast taken upon thineself to do - then I shall give unto thee Greater responsibility -- And it shall be given unto thee to be prepared to receive it -- For this have I given unto thee this Mine Work For this have I given of Mineself - Mine Love, Mine Energy that ye might come into the fullness of thine Stature.

So be it - I AM Sananda

Recorded by Sister Thedra of the Emerald Cross

Beloved Ones - While it is yet time, let it be said that the Way of the Lord hast not been fully revealed unto man -- I say "man" sees only in part the Plan -- And for this does he wonder - for this is he bewildered, for he hast set himself apart and considered himself a thing separate - at times thought himself sufficient unto his own --

Now it is come when he shall Know he is not self-sufficient - he shall Ask for assistance - for he shall Know he is not alone - and therefore does not stand alone -- He shall be as One and as such he shall Seek the help of the other parts which Makes up the Whole - which is the Body of the - and he shall be satisfied -- He shall be as One with All other parts and he shall find strength therein - for he shall K<u>no</u>w he is not alone in his time of trials --

Trials there shall be - and the body of this "Great and Mighty Assembly" shall be as his shield - for they shall be with him and be as Brothers - fortuned to Know his every need. He shall find his hand strengthened - he shall find his footsteps sure - and his heart gladdened - for his strength shall be certain -- He shall endure the storms and the suffering - for he shall Know wherein he is staid -- So let it be that thine hand shall be in Mine and I shall lead thee unto the summit - wherein ye shall <u>See</u> wherein ye have been - and Know unto which ye shall Attain.

So be it and Selah --

I AM the Most Worthy

Grand Master

Recorded by Sister Thedra of the Emerald Cross

IT SHALL BECOME PART OF THEE

Beloved Ones -- There are none amongst thee which hast seen the Glory of the Lord -- Yet I say unto thee - that which hast not been seen shall be seen -- For it shall become part of thee -- And ye shall walk in the Light which is His ---

Ye shall know as He knows -- Ye shall <u>know</u> that ye <u>know</u> for the veil shall be removed - and ye shall <u>see</u> and <u>know</u> thine self TO BE -- and that is the Greater Part -- Ye shall BECOME - and ye shall no longer "think" thineself separate from Him -- For this do I speak unto thee this day -- Ye shall walk with surety - and ye shall be as one which knows thine TRUE IDENTITY - and from whence thou hast come - and whither thou goest -- I say ye shall <u>BEcome</u> aware of thine <u>true identity</u> - and ye shall be glad -- So be it I Am Come that ye know -- While it is as yet not revealed unto thee - I say it shall be - Be ye as ones prepared - for it is come when ye shall pick up thine feet - and come into the place wherein I Am - and ye shall find therein Great Light and it shall not blind thee -- So be it - I have given of Mineself that ye be prepared - Let it be ---

I AM Sananda

Recorded by Sister Thedra of the Emerald Cross

Instructions - To the Messengers

While it is now the time for thine next part, I say unto thee: let thine hand be swift to give unto them this Mine Word - and it shall bless them which are of a mind to receive it -- While it is not given unto all to be of a mind to receive it - it is for the ones which will - and they shall be blest ---

Whereupon I shall be bound by Mine Love unto them -- I shall give unto them as they are prepared to receive -- While it is given unto Me to be One of the Council which now sits in Council for the benefit of ALL - I say it behooves ME to say unto thee that I Am not of the nether world -- Neither AM I of the "dead" --

I Am One of the Council which hast never been within the Earth -- born of woman -- Never have I taken upon Mineself the vehicle of flesh. Yet - I say unto thee - it is none-the-less that I Am as man - and as One with Mine Father -- For I AM as One bound by Love only --

And for this reason do I speak out this day -- When it is given unto One of the Host to speak - it carries a variation of vibrations - and each unto its own - each unto his own -- For each has a part for thee -- Each adds his part - his blessing -- And for this do We reach out that all might be blest --

Yet not all have the mind to accept that which We proffer -- Wherein is it said that they which are of a MIND to receive shall receive. Now I say unto thee -- When they refuse to accept the "WORD" - ye shall let them be -- Be ye not dismayed - nor be ye downcast for their unknowing -- Let them be ---

Be ye no part of their foolishness-- Forch not thine part upon them, for therein is foolishness -- Let them come of their own will -- It is said: "Seek Ye The Light And It Shall Not Be Denied Thee" -- So be it Truth.

For many stand by to assist thee -- Accept Mine blessing - and be ye glad for thine receiving ---

I AM -

Recorded by Sister Thedra of the Emerald Cross

The Motivating Force of the Council
Brotherhood of the White Star

Be ye as Mine hand and give unto them this Mine Word -- And let it be known that there is but One Council of the Great and Might - which is the <u>Ruling</u> <u>Council</u> for ALL the Schools of Light -- For ALL the Brotherhoods of Man -- The LOVE which IS - which WAS - is the MOTIVATING Force of this Council wherein We serve SELFLESSLY - and without thot of reward ---

Wherein is it said: "To Serve Is The Greatest of Joy" -- To give of One's self is the GREATEST REWARD -- So be it that We of the Brotherhood of the White Star - have served long and without self-recognition -- While We know Ourself to be One with The Father - We give no thot of "Self" as such. We have no thot of self-gain - profit - or any desire what-so-ever to enmesh any man within a net/ web - by any dogmas - creeds or doctrines -- We but ask of thee adherence unto the law which is set forth -- And by application of such law - ye shall become liken unto the Sons of God -- And ye shall walk with Them - Ye shall know Them and be One with Them -- So be it that to KNOW is WISDOM ---

When it is said: "Ye Shall Know Them" - it shall be revealed unto thee that which They are -- For many wear the veil of secrecy - which shall be torn away -- So be it that I speak unto thee that ye be prepared to receive One which shall come -- Yet he shall wear the garments of flesh -- He shall K<u>no</u>w himself to be One with Us -- Wherein is it said "To Know is Wisdom?" --

I say he shall <u>not</u> call himself wise. Yet he shall know for a surety that he hast come for a purpose and that purpose shall be done - and carried out to the completion -- For he knows what he is about -- He hast not betrayed himself -- For that matter he shall not -- For he is NOT a traitor -- So be it I have spoken that ye be prepared to receive him -- Let it be so ---

I AM One of the Council

Sing ye a sweet song - and be ye glad that this day is <u>Come.</u>

For I say the day bringeth forth Great Light and much rejoicing ---

So Be It

Recorded by Sister Thedra of the Emerald Cross

First and Second Creation
Sons of God -- Sons of Perdition

Beloved Ones -- While it is yet time - let it be understood that the Allwise - Almighty Father has ALL POWER -- And HE is that which IS - EVER WAS - and SHALL EVER BE - Worlds without end --

While the worlds might end - HE shall endure -- Now for that matter - thou art ONE in HIM - of HIM -- Thou art <u>not</u> <u>Him</u> - for He is the sum total of ALL which there is -- He is the WHOLE - and from out THIS WHOLE -- From out the ALL - thou art caused to BE -- Yet thou hast conditioned that which thou hast brot into thine own world of existence by thine experiences which thou hast fortuned unto thineself -- So be it that there is not one man which liveth - which is not included within the WHOLE.

Yet let it be understood - that there are ones which doth but appear to be alive - Which are not alive - Which are but animated - and which are not eternal beings -- Which hast not come from out the Whole -- These are but the Second Creation - which are not of the first - for the second shall not be capable of Eternal Life - for they are not of the Light and are not capable of receiving or comprehending it -- These are the "Sons of Perdition" which shall be cast into outer darkness -- For they shall be known for that which they are - They are not capable of that which is called "Life"- For when the illusion passes - the form - that which hast animated it --

For the thot which hast brot it forth as a "Spore" hast - or shall be withdrawn and be as nothing -- So it hast been So it shall be - for a time. And the time is now come when these "Spores" and "Whores" shall be no more -- For the "Whore" is the One which creates the Spores and that which is <u>imperfect</u> -- Let it be understood - that the whore is the thot which brings into manifestation that which is unreal - that which takes form - and that which is fed - and animated by the thots of men -- I say that the thots of men - in the "world of men" - has become the "Black Dragon" which lies in wait to devour them ---

While he hast no power over thee - I say it behooves Me to tell thee that he is of <u>Great</u> <u>Strength</u> - and he is fed - fattened and kept alive by that which man feeds/gives unto him ---

I say: Give unto him <u>nothing</u> which shall enable him to survive -- Let him die of starvation -- Have no mercy upon him - for he has no mercy upon thee --

He lies ready to devour the child - the aged - the very Host yea - he would even devour -- I say be ye no part of his survival!! ---

I Am come that ye might know the "Real" from the false. So be it I have spoken for the good of All -- Yet some shall deny Mine Words. Yet others shall know them for that which they are -- They are designed to free them from bondage ---

I say: These Mine Words are designed to eliberate them which are held in bondage by the dragon -- So be it they shall turn unto the Light, seek the Light/Truth - and they shall ask of the Father for Truth - and it shall not be hidden from them.

I say: They shall ask of no man "his" opinion -- They shall keep their own council - and be diligent in their search for Truth -- Waver not - and no man can take them captive ---

I AM One of the Great and Mighty Council -

Recorded by Sister Thedra of the Emerald Cross

The Times Shall Try Man's Spirit

Behold Me the Lord thy God -- Behold in Me the Light which I AM -- See ye that which I shall do -- Know ye that there is much to be done And great shall be the accomplishment.

Now ye shall go forward as One with Me - knowing that thou art not alone - that thou hast a part within the "Plan"- and there is "A Host" which stands ready to assist thee -- Let not thine feet weary - for I say unto thee - the way is steep and the climb arduous - and not one is without direction -- Yet ye shall <u>heed</u> that <u>direction</u> ---

When it is come that they weary of the climb - they wait. For I say unto thee - they which weary go not forth as ones prepared -- They wait, for they are frail of spirit - and they weary easily ---

Yet the times shall try man's spirit - and demand of him his ALL - Yet he shall give his ALL -- For the fulfillment shall be as accomplished -- While they which ask for self a puny pittance - shall find that they are blinded by their own self-created veil -- They shall see but that which they have created for themself - knowing not that the Light is theirs for the most part - that the Light is Present - <u>ever present</u> And it is that for which they seek -- For therein is ALL THINGS which is REAL and GOOD -- For <u>Good</u> and <u>evil</u> are opposite -- GOOD is REAL - ETERNAL --

Evil is darkness and fades with the Light -- It is un-reality -- And not one which has the mind to learn can be misled - or mistake one for the other -- For it is clearly stated - "Ye shall see the Light and it shall not be hidden" -- So be it that ALL things shall be revealed in the Light, For therein is NO darkness -- For the darkness is that which doth <u>appear</u>

to be - while it is but the illusion - it shall pass. The True - the Real - shall remain -- So let it be -- For therein is not anything hidden - and the false shall no more appear to be Real -- So be it that I have spoken of the GOOD - the evil - True and the false.-

I AM Sananda

> **Recorded by Sister Thedra of the Emerald Cross**

Thine Sole Concern

Beloved Ones -- It is said that the way of the Initiate is not an easy one.- Yet it is said that the way is now open before thee -- While it is yet time I say unto thee - hear ye this: and <u>know</u> ye that it is not afar off when ALL that hast been said shall be unto thee thine armor - thine strength in the time of need -- I say that the "Sibors" have sibored thee well -- And at no time have WE left anything <u>unsaid</u> which should be of any concern unto thee --

For thine preparation is <u>thine sole concern</u> at this time -- Wherein is it said that this is the <u>Day</u> of <u>Preparation</u> -- Wherein art thou weak? Wherein art thou strong? -- I say unto thee take ye heed of thine strength and know that thou art not sufficient unto thine self. <u>Ye shall avail thineself of</u> 'THIS HOUR' - <u>this day</u> - and be ye as ones alert -- Let not thine foot slip -- For I say unto thee - the way is steep - the climb is not easy -- yet the overcoming is that which is meant by the ascent -- And the descent can be swift and by all accounts very sad So be it that it behooves Me to say unto thee - be ye alert and aware of Mine Words -

and give not the bitter cup unto thineself -- for I say ye shall drink thereof ---

Let it be --

I AM Sananda

Recorded by Sister Thedra of the Emerald Cross

Space Program (?)

Beloved Ones -- Wherein is it said that - "The Ones which <u>think</u> themself wise shall be brot low -" So shall it be - for they shall be brot up short -- And they shall not make a mockery of Mine Words - neither Mine Work ---

I say: They which doth make a mockery of Mine Words/Mine Work shall be brot up short -- So be it the law. For it is given unto Me to see them - running hither and yon seeking ways and means of being as ones free from the gravitation of the EARTH - and to reach the Moon.- Yet they have heeded not the law which would unbind them ---

I say: They have not heeded the law which would unbind them! So be it they shall come to know that they are bound by a law which is exacting - and they shall abide by it -- So be it that there are Ones which <u>know</u> - yet they strive NOT to break such law -- They are as ones which work with it - apply it - and use it for the <u>Good</u> of <u>ALL</u> --So be it I speak from the Great and Grand Council wherein We <u>Know</u> that "Good" - what is meant by "THE GOOD OF ALL" -- So be it that they shall first learn to <u>Love</u> <u>One</u> <u>Another</u> ---

Such is Mine Word this day ---

I AM Sananda

Recorded by Sister Thedra of the Emerald Cross

Clean It Out!!

I Wait - I Watch - I Speak -

Sori Sori --Let it be understood that the way hast been made clear - the door opened - and the law clearly stated -- And for this have We opened up the way - The Communion which is Ours - is the part which I have kept for this day -- The Communion which We share is but that which "they" seek - yet they have not the strength of character to follow where I lead them -- When it is understood that they prepare themself for to Commune with ME - it shall give unto Me great joy -- For I wait, I watch - I speak -- They move not -- They have the same hatred - the same self-pity - the same legiron - and these I abhor! -- So be it I say - Go into thy secret place and rid thineself of all thine self-pity --

All thine preconceived ideas of Me and Mine Work --of the idols thou hast fashioned -- Rid thineself of all thine conceit and hypocrisy - and forget not that I see and know thee - and thine weakness -- I say rid thineself of all thine legirons!! - Make ye haste to cleanse out thine closet wherein thou hast buried the rubbish! - I say rubbish!! -- For it does not profit thee to hold on to it -- Cleanse it out -- Let it be no part of thee - When this is done - I shall commune with thee and ye shall sup from Mine Cup ---

So be it - I AM Sananda

The Lord thy God --

Recorded by Sister Thedra of the Emerald Cross

To the Weak and Poor in Spirit

Sananda

Let it be said this day that the way is made strait - the way clear -- And many stand by to assist thee -- Ye it is necessary to give thine ALL, for none shall do thine part for thee -- Yet it is for this that I say: "Blest is he which is prepared for the next part" - for it is said - "from Glory to Glory" and it is so ---

When thou hast attained the "Summit" - Ye shall find more Glorious fields afar which shall beckon unto thee -- I say unto thee: COME! COME! Arise with me and I shall lead thee into far fields ye know not of -- Yet the chains of bondage shall be cut away and be no more -- I say the chains which bind thee shall be cut away! -- And ye shall be the One to cut thineself loose - I say - "Ye shall cut away thine OWN legirons - for none other shall take them from thee" -- Some cherish them - and use them as if they were Great and Glorious instruments of mercy - of Great Love and Compassion - excusing themself their weakness ---

I SAY: CUT THEM AWAY! - Use them not to excuse thine weakness! -- Be ye free from them -- Hide not thine frailties beneath the garments of flesh ---

I say: -- These thine weaknesses are not of the flesh - they are within thineself - thine character -- I say "Build for thineself the mansion for tomorrow" ---

Let thine weakness be overcome -- Arise and behold the way which I point -- I say be ye as ones prepared to follow Me - Come! I shall direct thee -- Yet ye shall have the STRENGTH OF CHARACTER to go where I lead thee ---

I have spoken unto the weak and the poor in spirit -- Let them have this Mine Word -- For it is designed to prepare them for Greater things.-

I AM Sananda

Recorded by Sister Thedra of the Emerald Cross

To Parents ---
Present Generation ---

Beloved Ones -- When it is come that thine eye is opened ye shall see that there are no barriers unto Us - for Us - Neither do We create them. They are created by the law -- And the law prohibits any one which-so-ever passing into the Holy of Holies unprepared -- For it is the law that as one prepares himself - so does he receive ---

Let it be said - that one can have his choice wherein he abides -- He may choose his abiding place -- Yet he hast not learned that the Greater Part awaits him -- He hast not fortuned unto himself the Greater Part.

For the most part - he has not known that he is responsible for his condition -- for his plight -- I say he is responsible -- And woe unto any man which misuses his energy to bind his fellow man -- I say woe unto him -- While the Just shall be blest - I say the "wrongdoer" shall be his own worst enemy - Such is man's responsibility unto himself ---

Now let it be understood that there are ones unresponsible and these are the responsibility of the society - of the ones which have such responsibility -- And the law says: - They shall be as ones responsible for themself - and for the unresponsible -- For it is given unto the "Guardians of Truth and Justice" to uphold the law - that the innocent suffer not - I say: The Guardians of Truth and Justice shall uphold the law - with their very life -- And they shall be as ones rewarded ---

I say - Great is their responsibility -- For when they are true unto their trust - they are servants of the Law -- And there is Justice within the Law -- Let it be said that when the guardians of the Child are responsible for themself - They likewise - and for this - are they responsible for their offspring -- I say the child knows not what he shall do - for his mind is not mature -- His memory blanked from him -- With no parental direction is a sorry plight -- I tell thee - the parent which is "Self responsible" has the responsibility of the child upon his shoulders until the child hast become accountable - until he hast learned the law. And that he hast the will to abide thereby -- So be it that I have spoken to the parents of a wayward generation - wherein are many prophets - many leaders - many yet to be unveiled -- Many which shall lead thee unto Greater horizons -- These shall be the "Pioneers" - The "Trail Blazers" -- To them I say -- AWAKEN!!! --- So be it - I AM Sananda

Recorded by Sister Thedra of the Emerald Cross

Self pity - Escape - Suicide

Of all the ages this age shall bring forth Greater <u>things</u> - Greater revelations - and Greater progress -- That which hast seemed to be progress shall be as naught in comparison -- While it is not yet apparent unto thee the end -- It is now apparent that ye shall come to know the end -- And the end of <u>this</u> age shall indeed be a Glorious one - for it shall end in a Glorious and Glad awakening -- I Am come that it be so.- So shall it be -- For it is so decreed this day!

I bring unto thee Light which is of a Greater density -- It is of a Greater density - and it shall be the fulfilling of Mine Word unto thee. I have said - "I shall do Mine Part that ye be prepared for the Greater Part" -- So be it -- And it is now given unto Me to be One of the Host - and no man shall close Me out -- For I Am not bound by their might/power of thinking -- I come that they be unbound -- So let them which seek freedom from bondage - seek the Light - and ask of the Father - and they shall not be denied ---

So be it that it is now come when they shall spill their own blood in fear and confusion - with the thot that it end their confusion - their misery -- Yet I say unto them which seek escape from the law -- Behold thineself still! -- Behold thineself in thine misery still -- Behold thineself in the environment which thou hast created for thyself -- I say: Behold thine environment - and know ye that thou hast created it ---

Be ye as the one prepared to bring forth that which thou hast prepared thineself for to have - for to see - for to know - I have spoken unto them which have given unto themself the "Bitter Cup" -- Let it be understood that the ones which prepare for themself the "Bitter Cup" shall drink to the last - the dregs thereof ---

I say: There is no escape - for the law is explicit and knows no bounds -- It is eternally the <u>law</u> - and final -- No man sets it aside - or makes it void -- The "hope" of man is the application and the preparation for the Greater Part -- So be it that they which spill their own blood are more prone to self-pity and weakness of character -- So be it they too shall learn - for there is no place wherein they might hide.- Life IS - and there is NO END - NO BEGINNING - And for this I say COME ye FORTH and ARISE FROM THE "PIT" and <u>become</u> <u>As</u> <u>One</u> <u>Alive</u> -- Fortune unto thineself no darkness So be it Mine Word hast gone out upon the eth - and it shall be heard - and it shall bless them which hath heard --- I AM.

Recorded by Sister Thedra of the Emerald Cross

Faith

While it is time - let it be said that as there are the ones which see and know - while there are others which walk blindly - seeing not whither they goest -- Yet it is said "Blest is he which follows Me - for I shall lead him into fields he knows not of" ---

I shall bring him out of bondage - and I shall bring him into the place of Mine abode wherein there is no bondage -- So shall they which have the WILL to follow Me be glad for their preparation -- So be it I have decreed it so ---

While <u>they</u> walk blindly - I SEE - and I walk before them that the way be made clear before them -- I Am the Wayshower - and I go before them - for I have gone this way before - and I Know ---

So be it that they which follow Me shall find that their waiting shall end -- And they shall find that they have come unto the end of their waiting - and it shall be a glad day! ---

I say: Behold the Glory of the Lord -- For it is come when I shall make Mineself known unto them which are prepared to receive Me -- For this have I spoken out this day -- So let it be heard in ALL the lands and on the waters - "I AM COME" - "I AM COME" - I AM COME" - So be it they which are prepared to receive Me shall be made to SEE and KNOW ME ---

So be it and Selah -- I AM Sananda

Recorded by Sister Thedra of the Emerald Cross

Behold the New Day & Rejoice

Beloved Ones -- Mine hand I raise in supplication this day - And with this I say unto thee - "Behold the New Day and rejoice -- For it brings with it a new Work - a new Word - a new Part -- And no part is small - for all parts are of <u>great</u> consequence - and fit into <u>One</u> <u>Harmonious</u> <u>Whole</u> ---

I say - there are <u>no</u> small or insignificant parts within the Whole - for they are ALL part of the Whole ---

Now wherein is it said that to receive Me is to receive Mine Word To reject Mine Word is to reject Me -- For I AM - and for <u>that</u> is the Word -- And at no time have I given unto thee a part without cause -- There is Wisdom in the Parts which I give - and <u>no</u> part is to be discounted -- So let it be that I have given unto thee all that is sufficient unto thine salvation -- I say - Let thine time be spent in seeking out the Light which I bring -- Which I AM -- And let thine hands be swift to do Mine Work -- Mine mind is the mind which shall be thine mind - and with this shall ye comprehend the Work which I shall do - thru them which are Mine Flock -- I say: "Mine Flock" - for these are the ones which hear that which I say and follow Me - unto the end -- So be it I have spoken and thou hast heard Me ---

I bless thee -- I say: "Blest are they which hear that which I say" -- So be it - I AM

Sananda

Recorded by Sister Thedra of the Emerald Cross

Hypocrisy & Results

Such is Mine Word unto thee this day -- And let it be understood - that when one professes to follow Me - and uses Mine Name for his own use - for his own gain - or vain sayings - he shall be brot low -- For I say unto them: "Thou shall not take the Name of The Lord God in vain" "Thou shall not take the Name of the FATHER - SOLEN AUM SOLEN - vainly" - or speak it lightly - for it is the MOST SACRED OF ALL NAMES ---

So let it rest Sweet upon thine lips and give unto HIM All the Praise and the Glory -- I AM the SON SENT that ye might KNOW HIM - The FATHER Which hast sent ME ---

So be it - I say - the Name of SOLEN AUM SOLEN is the SWEETEST of ALL NAMES -- So let it rest Sweetly upon thine lips - and be ye blest ---

I AM Sananda

> **Recorded by Sister Thedra of the Emerald Cross**

I am Therefore Qualified
... One of the Council

Beloved Ones -- While it is given unto Me to be One of the Council which has the fortune to <u>know</u> that which goes on within the realm of Light -- I Am therefore qualified to say unto thee that "The way of the transgressor is hard" -- That the way is now open for the Candidate which has the WILL to attain -- For there are many which stand by to give assistance -- Yet he - the Candidate shall be obedient unto the law He shall expect <u>no</u> <u>favors</u> - no exception -- He shall be as the one to find his own way -- He shall come by his own will - his own effort - his own attainment -- He shall not lean upon his fellow man - neither shall he attempt to emulate him. He shall be <u>himself righteous</u> - and clean -- He shall be unto himself true -- He shall endure all his trials with a grateful heart - knowing that it is his and not his brothers overcoming - He shall resist not his trials - rather be in a position to stand them - overcome them -- For it is his endurance which shall profit him -- For his weakness profit him naught ---

It is said - to overcome self is the preparation which is necessary to attain -- So be it the law -- Self is the <u>deceiver.</u> It is the self which hears that which the dragon sayeth - that which he wills thee to do -- It is the "self" which would yield unto his promptings - and whisperings -- When he would use thee - he first would appeal to thee thru the lower self - the appetites - the feeling world - the sensuous world - the world of form -- The feeling which thou hast for thine Beloved Ones - is but a puny counterpart of that which WE have for thee -- For I say unto thee - thou hast wandered far afield -- Now We see thee struggling to return unto thine abiding place - from whence thou hast gone forth - as a projection of this Realm - this Light -- Yet it is for this - that we reach out that ye might <u>know</u> thine TRUE-self - that ye might not be deceived. Now ye shall be glad for the assistance which WE offer -- So be it - I AM One which stands by -- I Am with thee that ye be blest this day -- So let it be ---

Recorded by Sister Thedra of the Emerald Cross

The Dragon's Magic

Beloved Ones -- It is said that - "To Know is Wisdom" -- Let it be well with thee - that ye <u>know</u> -- For this do We say - be ye aware of US - the Ones which keep Guard/Keep Watch. I say: We sleep not! Neither do We betray Our trusts -- We keep Guard - and We know that which goes on about thee - and within the 'world of men' for that matter ---

So be it -- We say - Keep thine own council - ask no favors, be ye as ones self-responsible -- Let not thine tongue betray thee - or trip thee up - for it is the weapon most effective unto the dragon -- <u>He makes good use of it</u>!!

Be ye aware - and know ye that he has <u>no</u> preference - NO scruples He is unjust and unashamed -- He has no ethic -- He performs miracles before their eyes - that he entrap them - that he hold them bound - that he hold them <u>spell-bound</u>! - that he give them their sights and wonders that he might have them as his pawn -- He distracts them from that which <u>I</u> give unto them ---

I say:- I say! -They run hither and yon - seeking out them which can show them MIRACLES which can hold them "spell-bound" ---

So be it I say unto them: "Seek ye the Light --- and ALL THINGS shall be added unto thee/given unto thee to know".- So be it and Selah.-

I AM Sananda - the Lord thy God

                    Recorded by Sister Thedra of the Emerald Cross

So be it I have Spoken of 'Dedication'

Beloved Ones -- What is the time other than now? Where is the future? What is the yesteryear? I say there is but the NOW -- And what dost thou expect of the MORROW? -- I say unto thee -this moment is thine to do with as ye will -- So be it that ye shall cherish it -- And be glad for THIS MOMENT -- Do with it as ye will - for it is thine -- Yet let it hold for thee <u>Great</u> <u>Joy</u> and <u>Praise</u> -- Be ye glad for it -- Rest not on the yesteryears - for they are gone - and shall be no more -- While it is now come that ye shall be dedicated unto the Work at hand - I say rejoice in it -- Rejoice for thine part Any part given unto thee to do - for there are many parts - and NO part is trivial - no part menial in Mine House --

I say unto thee - Mine Servants call themselves <u>Servants</u> and they are glad for their parts - however small -- So be it I give unto them as they are wont to receive -- It is the law -- As they give so shall they receive -- And it is the joy of giving that counts -- So be it that I have spoken unto thee of dedication - and of Service unto Me - unto the Plan.

So be it I AM Sananda

Recorded by Sister Thedra of the Emerald Cross

Eternal I Say!

Behold in Me the Light Which I AM -- Behold in Me the Light Which thou art -- Behold in Me - the Life - the Way - the Truth - And sing ye paeans of praise unto the Father which hast given of Himself that we have Being - for in Him We have Our Being ---

I say: "WITHIN HIM We have Our Being"-- So be it that I KNOW, for I <u>know</u> Mineself to Be One with the Source of Being -- So be it I reveal Mineself unto thee that ye too might come to <u>know</u> as I <u>know</u> -- This is My Mission - <u>Mine</u> <u>Task</u> that ye be brot out of bondage ---

While it is yet given unto thee to be <u>as</u> ones bound by flesh, I say unto thee: - flesh can <u>not</u> bind thee - for thou <u>Art</u> <u>Eternal</u> ETERNAL I say! -- ETERNAL BEINGS art thou ---

Arise as ones come forth from the tomb - and walk ye as one Alive And hold up thine head -- Let not thine feet drag, neither thine heart fail thee -- For I say unto thee - thou art of the First-born ---

Born of God the Father art thou - and at no time hast He taken from thee thine inheritance - which He hast Willed unto thee -- Thou hast but to claim it in His Name ---

So be it I raise Mine hand in Holy Benediction - and I proclaim thee Sons of God -- So be it and Selah -- I AM He which is sent that ye might come into the fullness of thine inheritance -- So be it as thou hast willed it ---

I AM Sananda

Recorded by Sister Thedra of the Emerald Cross

I Say: "Let There Be Light!!"

Beloved Ones -- When it is come that thou art given thine freedom from bondage - ye shall know that which thou hast not remembered in the time of thine bondage -- Ye shall have thine memory restored unto thee for in that place wherein ye shall GO ye shall have thine memory -- There shall be no mystery - no darkness - no bondage ---

Yet I say unto thee - not ALL shall be so fortuned -- For unto them which deny the Word and heed not the LAW - I say unto them: Let not thine mind deceive thee -- Let not thine opinions trip thee up -- For all is not as thou hast fashioned -- All is not well -- For it behooves ME to tell thee that there are many places of abode - each fashioned differently and according unto the degree of Light which they can bear ---

I say each shall be put into his own environment - wherein he shall be at one with it -- He shall be in the place like unto that which he hast fashioned for himself -- He shall do well to seek the Light -- His freedom depends upon him - his own <u>will</u> -- He puts forth the <u>will</u> to serve the Light -- And he puts from him all his puny ways - his selfishness - his own puny <u>will</u> - that the Father's Will be done in him thru him - and by him -- He has none other will -- Unto him I say: "All things shall be added unto thee for thine own Good" - So be it and Selah I Am come that there be Light - LIGHT! LIGHT!! - I Say: LET THERE BE LIGHT!!!

So be it I AM Sananda

Recorded by Sister Thedra of the Emerald Cross

When Shall We See the Fullness of the Plan?

Sarah Speaking: - Such is Mine Word unto thee this day -- When it is given unto thee to know the fullness of "The Plan" then ye shall see that it is fashioned by and thru the LOVE which WE bear thee ---

When thou hast been unbound - that ye see as ones unbound - <u>then</u> ye shall see the fullness of <u>The</u> <u>Plan</u>/see without limitation -- <u>Then</u> ye shall <u>know</u> - and <u>know</u> that ye Know! -- I too tell thee <u>this</u> <u>day</u> - that <u>everything</u> is according unto the law -- Everything! ---

There is NO escape from "The Law" - for to be one with it is the power of Love -- To be in discord with it is the opposite -- I say - to LOVE as WE LOVE is the thing -- To Know as WE Know comes from obedience unto the Law ---

For in the day when thou didst go into bondage - it was for the reason of deliverance - for them which had transgressed the law -- Yet thou hast taken up the veil - and taken upon thineself the condition known as sleep ---

For thou hast had thine memory blanked from thee -- Thou hast not remembered Me -- Thou hast not remembered thine Source -- While it is said: "Let there be Light" - there IS LIGHT -- Now We say: "Be ye as Ones Awakened unto thine Divinity" - and know ye that thou art Sons of God - and <u>Divine</u> in thine Source --- While it is said that there are ones which are not Divine in origin -- These are "The Sons of Perdition" ---

So be it that I have said unto thee - "<u>All</u> <u>is</u> <u>not</u> <u>well</u>"- it is so -- For it is now come when the Sons of God shall make war on the Sons of Perdition -- And they shall have no power over the <u>Sons of God</u> ---

I tell thee: The Sons of Perdition shall persecute the Sons of God - and they shall be merciless in the doing -- They shall have no scruples for they are under the banner of the <u>Skull and Crossbones</u> ---

I tell thee: WATCH! LOOK! SEE! - and KNOW them for that which they are -- Give unto them NO power over thee - for thou art called out from amongst them -- Thou hast been given a talent - and it shall be multiplied a thousand fold -- Let not their deceit and guile touch thee -- For I Am thine shield and thine armor -- I Am thine Everlasting and Eternal Mother - which holds thee within the Everness of Mineself - So be it I have kept thee thru the days of thine <u>Un-Knowing</u>. So be it I AM the Mother Eternal -

Recorded by Sister Thedra of the Emerald Cross

Awareness - Of Thine Divinity

Art thou not aware of thine Self -- Art thou not aware of Being -- Art thou not aware of thine Divinity? -- I say unto thee - because thou art Divine thou dost have thine Being within the Father Which hast sent thee forth as part of Himself – as the hand - the foot extended -- He hast the power and the will to move it forth - to bring it back - to do that which He will with that which He hast sent forth ---

As thou dost stretch forth thine hand of thine own 'free will' - thou art able to withdraw it - thrust it forward and withdraw it -- Therein is motion and energy - set into motion of thine own will -- Now I say unto thee - the <u>Father</u> hast sent thee forth as Himself - as one made flesh - and as one projected of Himself - And He shall bring thee forth as He <u>wills</u> -- For it is His Will that ye be at One with Him -- And at no time hast thou been separate from Him -- Yet thou hast not been <u>aware</u> of thine Source - the Source of thine Being.-

It is now come when ye shall become aware of thine Divinity -- And ye shall be glad - for it is thine "Salvation" - I say unto thee it is thine deliverance from bondage - thine own unknowing - which hast bound thee in darkness -- So be it I say unto thee: "Be ye aware of thine Divinity" - for it is given unto thee to be Eternal Beings - and of Divine origin.

For this have I spoken unto thee - that ye might <u>Know</u> - that ye might become <u>aware</u> of thine Source -- So let it be for thine own sake that I say unto thee: "Awaken Unto Thine True Identity"---

Recorded by Sister Thedra of the Emerald Cross

Sanandas Word

Beloved Ones -- Let this day bring forth the fulfillment of the 'WORD" "Let there Be Light"-- Let the WORD be unto thee thine word -- Let it be unto thee sufficient -- Now it is said - that the Word shall be sufficient unto thine salvation -- So shall it be - for it carries with it the POWER of SALVATION, the power of fulfillment -- And at no time shall it fail thee -- Yet ye shall accept it for that which it is -- Ye shall be as Ones prepared to go the last mile -- And for that hast it been said: "When thou hast given thine ALL unto the Plan - and followed ME - then thou shall know" - for it is given unto thee to be walking as ones bound in flesh -- Yet it is said - flesh shall not bind thee longer - that is when it is finished and thou hast finished thine mission -- And THEN ye shall be as ones freed from the Wheel of rebirth - and never again shall ye be born of woman - I say unto thee - Let it be fulfilled -- For such is the WORD I give unto thee this day -- And Mine Word is the Law - Mine Word is the Truth and the Life -- For I AM the Life/ the Way -- For this have I said: "FOLLOW YE ME"---

And ye shall be filled with joy -- Accept - Mine Blessings and Know ye that ye are Not Alone --

I AM Sananda

Recorded by Sister Thedra of the Emerald Cross

Aggression & Oppression

Beloved Ones -- While it is yet time - let it be said that all is not well within the realm of man --For he is rebellious and filled with fear -- He has not the will to follow where I lead - where I point -- He is a rebellious lot -- Man is the only creature which has free will upon the Earth -- Yet he has misused the energy allotted unto him - that he be put into such as he has now found himself confronted with -- I say his lot is a sad one indeed! He hast truly portioned out for himself a bitter cup -- When he hast drunken the last bitter dreg he shall be as one prepared to seek the assistance which We proffer -- I say unto them which have a mind to follow Me - be <u>ye</u> No part of their foolishness - and give unto them credit for being the fools which they are ---

I say the WAR MONGERS - the Ones which OPPRESS Mine people - the ones which hold bound the ones which WOULD serve ME shall be put into a place wherein they too shall be bound -- So be it I have spoken out - and I Am not finished -- Let it be that I shall speak further on the subject of OPPRESSION and AGRESSION ---

I AM Sananda

Recorded by Sister Thedra of the Emerald Cross

I am the Governing Head
Serve Me

Beloved Ones: There is but One which has the Power and the Authority to bring thee out of the place wherein thou Art. That is the One which hast placed thee therein - which hast given unto thee the calling - and given unto thee the place - the time- and energy. And at <u>no</u> time shall ye be unto any man grateful for this part -- For I say unto thee it is by the effort and the wisdom - of this One which hast been unto thee thine shield - and thine buckler - that thou hast been placed within the place wherein thou art -- Thou hast prepared thineself to be brot therein - and for this wast it done-- Now I say <u>there</u> <u>are</u> ones which hast contributed unto the support of that place -- While they have asked for a part - it is their part to contribute thereto--

When it is said that there are ones which have given of their substance - and their energy - that Mine Work be accomplished - I say it is that which I have given unto them to do. So let them respond in like manner. And be ye not under bondage unto them -- For I say I Am the Director - and the Governing Head of this place - and activity and at <u>No</u> <u>time</u> shall I deny thee that which I have kept for thee -- I say thou art as one true unto thineself - and be ye not of a mind to grovel unto them for a pittance -- I say serve ME with thine whole heart - and mind and no man shall close thee out--

I say unto thee - none hast the Authority which I have -- And I have given unto thee Mine Cloak of Authority - and placed upon thee Great Responsibility -- So be it I know thy capacity - and I shall not give unto thee more than thou canst bear -- I AM with thee that ye might be Strengthened -- So be it I AM -

Sananda

Recorded by Sister Thedra of the Emerald Cross

Awaken unto Me

Beloved Ones -- It is with the "Word" that thou art sustained. I say the Word hast gone forth -- "Let there BE LIGHT" - and there IS Light --

See it and <u>Know</u> ye that there <u>is</u> Light - And at no time shall ye fall or faint by the way --- I say See and Know ye that I Am come that there Be Light - To Know is to Be -- To Be is to Know -- I say to <u>know</u> is thine Divine right -- Therefore I say unto thee - be ye as ones Aware of thine SOURCE - and Know ye that thou hast thine Being within ME - And for this do I say unto thee - thou art One with Me - and I Am not separate from thee -- I Am One with thee -- Ponder well these Mine Words - and I shall reveal many things unto thee ---

I say Awaken Unto Me -

The Lord thy God -

Sananda

Sanandas Blessings

Sori Sori-- Behold the hand of God move -- Know ye that it moveth -- And be ye as ones blest -- For it is given unto thee to be blest of Me - of Mine Presence - and by Mine Light ye shall walk -- So be it and Selah -- I say - by Mine Light ye shall walk -- Know ye that I AM - and because I AM - <u>thou</u> ART -- So be it that I Am with thee - that ye be blest ---

Rest thine hand in Mine and I shall lead thee gently - So gently - for I AM the Lord thy God -- Peace unto thee this day --

I AM Sananda

Recorded by Sister Thedra of the Emerald Cross

None Shall Know the Joy of Serving Until...

Beloved Ones -- None shall Know the joy of serving until they have given of themself -- Then they shall Know the Joy of selfless Service - For none other hast such joy -- Let it be said that selfless Service is that which brings joy unto the heart - that which is remembered -- I say ALL thine sorrow shall be forgotten - and thine selfless Service shall be thine Eternal Reward ---

Waste not thine time on the laggards -- Be ye no part of their selfishness -- Feed not them thine bread -- Let them be up and about their Salvation -- Let them not drink from thine cup -- Give unto them which thirst -- and feed them which doth hunger -- Yet I say ye shall not fill the bellies of thine enemies -- For they which are filled with deceit shall come with honeyed words of praise - and they would take of thine food and drink - and spit upon thee -- I say - these are filled with deceit -- Give unto them nought -- I say if they are not with thee - they are against ME --

Hear ye that which I say! I say: "They which are against thee are against ME" -- Give them nought which shall fill their bellies -- Let them go unfed Be ye no part of them - for they shall come - and they shall sit and question thee - They shall use the Word to their own use - and spit upon thee - I say: Woe unto any man which misuses Mine Word - or despises Mine Servant -- So be it that I have spoken -- Let them which have ears hear that which I say -- So be it I shall speak again and again - for I Am not finished --

I AM Sananda

Recorded by Sister Thedra of the Emerald Cross

Joy to the World the Lord is Come

Beloved of Mine Being --"Joy to the World The Lord Is Come" ---

Sing ye a glad song -- Let it fill thine heart -- Be ye as one filled with thanksgiving -- Let the Joyful news be Sounded thruout the land - Harken unto the Great and Mighty Host: "HE IS COME" - "HE IS COME" -- Come let Us rejoice together - for this is the time of rejoicing and <u>Work</u> -- There shall be Work aplenty -- And for this shall I fill thine hands to overflowing -- I say I shall fill thine hands to overflowing For there is WORK - and an abundance for all --

Yet it is given unto thee to have thine part allotted unto thee - thru the Mighty Council - which is the Council of Councils - the Head of ALL the Galactic Councils - the Council which is Over the Galactic Council -- And for this hast thou been prepared -- I say: It is given unto Me to be One of the Council - and none other hast the part which I shall allot unto thee -- So be it that the Way is now made clear - that We might give unto thee a Greater Responsibility -- For this do I speak at this time -- So be it I shall speak again – For this shall not be Mine last speaking -- Wait for a time then take up thine pen and write that which I say unto thee - and give it unto them which are of a mind to know that which I say -- And fortune unto thineself such Knowledge - as I have for thee--

So be it I AM- Sanat Kumara

Recorded by Sister Thedra of the Emerald Cross

The Greater Gift

Hold ye steadfast and I shall give unto thee a portion for them which shall profit them -- And they shall be glad for it -- Now say unto them which ask for Light - that they shall find - and at no time shall it be denied them ---

While it is given unto thee to be the hand of Me made manifest unto them - I say they shall be as ones willing to be led by the hand which is made manifest -- And at no time shall I give unto them that which they <u>Are</u> <u>Wont</u> <u>To</u> <u>Accept.</u> For it shall not be a part which is forched upon them -- They shall accept it of their own free will -- Yet I say: Blest are they which accept that which I proffer them -- Wherein is it said that I Am Sufficient Unto Mine Self? -- Yet I say - thou art Mine hand made manifest -- Have I not brot thee forth that it be so? -- Have I not given unto thee a Gift far Greater than Gold - OR ALL the Treasures of <u>theirs</u> - which they have treasured so watchfully? -- I say they think themself fortunate to have gold and silver - yet thine Gift far excels ALL their wealth - for they know not that which I have given unto thee ---

They seek greater wealth and greater freedom - yet they are bound by their legirons -- They know <u>not</u> freedom - they <u>are</u> <u>not</u> freed ---

They are bound by their own desires and wanting-- Their longing knows no bounds -- Wherein have they been satisfied? ---

I say unto them: They shall not be free from all bondage until they have given of themself - that they might serve Me selflessly -- And then they shall know Peace - for it shall be established within them -- While they talk of "Peace" - and of the "Path" - they know no peace - and they walk not The Path which I have walked -- For they have not the strength of character to follow where I lead -- For I say unto them "Come" - and they seek out strange gods - and question them concerning Mine Way.

I say they Know ME NOT! -- So be it I say unto them: Ye fools - which do make a mockery of Mine Words - MINE NAME -- I say Ye Know Me Not ---

So shall ye come to know the folly of thine hypocrisy - thine idolatry -- So be it I speak unto them which use Mine Name - knowing not that it is the One Given of the Father - that I might be known among men as THE ONE AND ONLY SANANDA-- Son of the Most High Living God Am I - and I Know Mineself to BE ---

So be it and Selah --

I AM Sananda

Recorded by Sister Thedra of the Emerald Cross

By Mine Grace Shall Ye Be Supplied

Beloved Ones -- While it is given unto Me to be thine Mother Eternal thou art Mine Children which I love and cherish as Mine own -- I am not unmindful of thee ---

I know thine every need -- For from Me cometh thine supply -- I have provided that which is necessary unto thine welfare -- So be it ye have but to accept it in Mine Name - and by Mine Grace shall ye be supplied ---

While it is thine part to accept it - and be glad for thine having the Source of Supply - close as thine hand and thine foot -- I say it is given unto Mine Children to want -- And they shall be as the ones which need not that which they want! -- These are the ones which know not that which they need -- Neither do they know the Source of their supply ---

I say unto thee - I Am the Source thru which ALL thine Supply cometh -- And it is given unto Me to be the Mother of ALL Manifestation which hast given unto thee comfort - and which thou has not recognized -- For it is given unto Mine Children to be unmindful of their many blessings -- So be it I have not forgotten them -- I ask that ye remember Me in thine days of labor - seeking - and working - wherein thou hast labored without thot of Me -- Let it be said that I Am the <u>Source</u> of thine Comfort -- "I AM THE COMFORTER" -- I Am One with the Father Eternal -- We know NO separation, We are One - We are <u>Not</u> divided -- So be it thou art One with ME -- And for that have I supplied thee - for I supply Mineself ---

I AM -

thine Mother Eternal

Recorded by Sister Thedra of the Emerald Cross

Ye Shall Not Drink Thereof

Behold the Lord thy God - and be ye blest -- Know that I Am with thee. For this have I come - that ye be blest -- While it is said that many shall give unto thee the bitter cup - I say unto thee - ye shall not drink thereof. For I shall give unto thee S<u>wee</u>t W<u>ate</u>r which they know NOT -- I say unto thee - be ye no part of their foolishness - and drink not of the cup which "they" have prepared for thee - Stand ye steadfast - falter not -- And give unto Me credit for Knowing that which goes on about thee -- I Am thine shield and thine buckler -- So be it I AM aware of the Plan of the -- and <u>of</u> men -- Man the lesser part -- The Greater part man hast not yet seen ---

Wait upon Me - the Lord thy God --

And I shall reward thee openly --

I AM Sananda

The Sibor of Sibors

Behold in Me the Light - The All Seeing One -

Behold in Me the Light which I AM -- And Know ye that thou Art One with Me -- And for this do I speak unto thee thusly ---

I say: Blest art thou - and blest shall ye be -- I say: "Behold In Me the Light Which I AM" -- And Know ye that I Am One with Mine Father Which hast sent Me -- So be it thou ART ONE WITH ME and I Am not separated from thee -- As it is written - "Mine Father and I Are One"- and thou Art One with Me -- So be it I speak that ye might Know that which I say -- Too - let it be said that I Am mindful of All that thou Art - or ever shall be ---

Now it is come when ye shall Come into the fullness of thine estate. And it is said: "All the Father has is thine" -- So be it and Selah ---

I AM with thee that it be so -- So let it Be – I AM Sananda

Recorded by Sister Thedra of the Emerald Cross

Most High Priest
Most Worthy Grand Master

Beloved Ones -- It is Mine part to say unto thee - there is the One which is known unto thee as the Most High Priest - and One known as the Most Worthy Grand Master -- Each has a part and a place -- And each is free to go and to come - and to be at any time - in any place what-so-ever -- He is not limited by time/space or material substance -- For He is Master of the MATTER - of the material substance-- Therefore he can take any form - and sort of substance - and He uses it for His Work which is to the Glory of the FATHER Which hast brot Us forth -- I say unto thee - these TWO are not as frail as man hast Imaged –

For They are Ones of Power and Authority - and are called "GODS"- and rightly so -- While it is Not said They are THE MOST HIGH LIVING GOD -Which is OUR FATHER which hast given unto Us Life / Being, I say: There is but One FATHER of US Which is known as SOLEN AUM SOLEN. And for this do I say unto thee: - Praise ye the Name of Solen Aum Solen -- And let it suffice that He is THE FATHER MOST HIGH and unto Him ALL the Praise and the Glory. While it is yet not come that ye KNOW the fullness of HIS BEING, I say unto thee: - Be ye as ones Mindful of HIM - and Be ye as ones prepared to see Him and to Know Him - as We Know HIM-- So be it and Selah. I have spoken unto thee that ye be blest this day ---

I AM Sanat Kumara

Recorded by Sister Thedra of the Emerald Cross

The Word Hast Gone Out - "Let There be Light"

Behold the Power of the Spoken Word -- See it made manifest -- I say unto thee: "See It Made Manifest" - and know ye this - that there is Power in THE WORD -- So let it be- for it is by the power of the Word that thou art sustained.

The WORD hast gone out: "Let there Be Light" - and there IS LIGHT -- So be ye One with it - and give unto it the Power that is due. Give unto thyself credit for knowing wherein thou art staid ---

I say - thou art One with the Light -- And <u>all</u> thine substance cometh from out the same Substance -- So be it - thou shall come to know from whence cometh thine sustenance - So be it that I Am One with IT -- Therefore I Know whereof I speak. Now ye shall be mindful of thine help -- And ye shall know from whence it cometh ---

I say - ye are the Sons of God - sent forth that there be Light in the world of men - wherein they labor for bread - wherein they grovel for a pittance -- So be it that ye shall walk knowing - and becomingly -- And I shall be unto thee ALL that ye shall have need of ---

So be it I AM the Lord thy God

Sananda

Recorded by Sister Thedra of the Emerald Cross

Who Shall He Lead?

Beloved Ones -- While it is yet time - let it be said that there are many which shall deny Me and Mine Word - and set foot against Mine people which have chosen to follow Me -- Yet it is said: "I shall not forsake them" -- For this do I say unto thee this day -- Follow ye Me - and I shall lead thee out of bondage ---

Yet ye shall choose Mine Way - for none other shall I lead. I Am come that ye be delivered out-- So let it be -- Wherein have I misled thee? -- Wherein hast thou found thine way? -- I ask of thee - wherein hast thou been sufficient unto thineself? Never was it so - for thou art not sufficient unto thine self - Thou art not alone -- For it is given unto Me to be One of the Mighty Host - which stands ready to assist thee ---

When it is come that ye have finished thine course - I shall direct thee upon thine next one - wherein thou shall know from whence thou came - to where thou Goest! -- When thou hast finished thine part within the realm of man - I shall bring thee forth as ones prepared for the Greater Part -- For this do I make Mine Pronouncements unto thee: Ask of no man his favor - Ask of no man his blessing -- Fortune unto thineself the blessing of the Mighty Host -- Stand ye steadfast - and will thine return unto thine Abiding Place - Place thine hand in Mine - and I shall lead thee -- For this have I extended Mine hand unto thee --Ye have but to accept it in Mine Name.

So be it I AM

Sananda

Recorded by Sister Thedra of the Emerald Cross

This is the Day for Which Thou Hast Waited

Beloved Ones -- This day I would say unto thee: Behold ye the hand of God move -- See it move - and know ye that there is none which shall stay it ---

It is come when it shall move swiftly - and with precision - and with great swiftness shall the things which have been foretold come to pass.

I say: These things which have been foretold from the <u>ages</u> <u>past</u> shall come to pass this day -- So let it be -- See the perfection of the law - and wait not for another day ---

I tell thee: THIS is the day for which thou hast waited -- Make ready thineself - for it is now come when Great things shall be accomplished within a short time ---

Time: - Time as ye know it - and reckon time -- There is no time other than the NOW -- Therefore WE say unto thee prepare thineself THIS DAY for that which ye shall become.

Wherein is thine hope -- Not in the 'morrow -- Yet it lies within <u>This</u> <u>Moment</u> -- I say unto thee: Seize it and cherish it and be ye as one blest -- Bless <u>this</u> <u>day</u> - and wait not for the morrow -- This is THE DAY for which thou hast waited ---

Listen unto Me -- Hear that which I say unto thee: - Give thine own self credit for being a Son of God the Father -- And give unto ME credit for K<u>nowing</u> that which I say unto thee.

Be ye blest thereby - for I shall reveal many things unto them which follow Me ---

Deceive not thineself - for I AM not deceived -- I Know Mine Own.

I Say: Come ye forth and be as One of Mine flock - and I shall lead thee into the "Secret Place of the Most High Living God"- for I Know the Way -- He and I are ONE -- So shall it ever Be --

I AM Sananda

Recorded by Sister Thedra of the Emerald Cross

I Say: 'Behold!'

Behold in Me the Light - The Light which I AM -- And behold in thineself the Light which thou Art -- Behold in thineself thine own Divinity - and be ye blest ---

I say: Behold in thine own self thine Divinity - and at no time shall it be hidden from thee ---

I say unto thee: See that which I shall show thee - and Know ye that thou ART ONE with ME -- I AM the Lord thy God - and I Am come that ye might <u>know</u> ---

I Say: I AM COME that ye might come to Know ---

So let it be -- For this have I revealed Mineself unto thee.

I AM Sananda

Recorded by Sister Thedra of the Emerald Cross

They Shall be Gathered Together

Beloved Children -- The time swiftly comes when the Sons of God shall be gathered together as One Body And therein shall be Great Power -- For there shall be no darkness within them -- They shall Know themself to be Sons of God -- And they shall have their memory as the Sons of God - And they shall be given that which is theirs by Divine Right -- They shall k<u>n</u>ow from whence they came - to where they go -- I say there shall be no mystery with or amongst them - for they shall be as O<u>n</u>e<u>s</u> C<u>o</u>m<u>e</u> A<u>live</u> -- They shall have no limitations neither shall they be bound by any law -- They shall be free of all law what-so-ever - for <u>they</u> <u>shall</u> <u>be</u> <u>the</u> LAW - and One with the Law of Love -- For the Law of Love covers All other law -- For <u>Love</u> is the fulfilling of the Law -- Wherein is it said: "'Love Ye One Another"- And it is the law which ye shall abide by -- And it shall profit thee -- I Am Come that ye might walk in the Light --

So be it - I AM - Sananda

      Recorded by Sister Thedra of the Emerald Cross

They are Filthy!

Beloved Ones -- This day I say unto thee - cry not for the ones which betray themself - for they alone are responsible for their betrayal -- They have been given the law - and the "Word" is clearly written - the law stated -- And it is given in thine language simple and plain - plainly stated! - That they might understand ---

Wherein is it said that "they which do betray themself shall be the saddest of the lot?"---

IT IS SO ----

I Am come that they know the law - that they be delivered from the 'fowlers snare' -- So be it they heed not that which I have said ---

I speak unto thee now - that ye be comforted - that ye be as ones prepared for that which shall be given unto thee to do. Ye shall be as ones alert-- Let not thine foot slip -- Let not their prattlings disturb thee. Let not their filth touch thee.

Be ye not contaminated by them - for I say they are filthy! -- Their tongues are given unto lies - and their hands are set to nefarious schemes -- I say they/shall cleanse themself - and offer up themself unto Me as a living sacrifice -- Then I shall give unto them that which I have kept for them -- So be it -- It is the Greater Part.

Rest ye in the Knowing - I Am thine shield and thine buckler ---

I Am with thee that ye be spared ---

So be it I AM -

Sananda

Recorded by Sister Thedra of the Emerald Cross

They Know Not the Import of "THE WORD"

Sori Sori -- Beloved of Mine Being -- Behold this day the Glory of the Lord -- Behold! See! And Know that ye are not alone -- I say - rejoice that ye are not alone!

Walk ye with surety - and be ye as one prepared to partake of Mine Cup -- For I shall give unto thee - that which I have for thee -- I Am fortuned to be the "Most Worthy Grand Master" - and I have given of Mineself that ye be freed from ALL thine legirons -- That ye be free to follow where the "MOST HIGH PRIEST" leads thee -- Let it be understood that there are ones which speak of things of Spirit - knowing not the meaning thereof --

The <u>Word</u> for instance -- They poll-parrot the words - yet they have not fathomed the depth of its meaning -- They have not the Strength of Character to follow where He leads -- He has given the law - and they have not been obedient unto it -- They give unto others the word as they have received it - while not applying it unto themself -- For they know not the Great import of "THE WORD". Let it be recorded that there are none exempt from the law -- Each shall be obedient unto it - thereby fulfilling it, the law -- And thru - and by obedience unto it do they find themself acceptable unto the Great and Mighty Assembly - the Grand Council - which hast directed - and protected them I say They have <u>direct</u>ed and <u>protect</u>ed them -- It Is So.

While they have gone headlong into the ditch -- I say WE of the Mighty Assembly - have sent into their midst Emissaries - that they might turn from the "ditch" - and not therein be entrapt -- So be it I have held out Mine hand unto them - that they might be prepared for the Greater part -- Yet they have not accepted it---

Let it be said - that ALL which are of a mind to accept it shall be blest thereby -- I come not to give a lengthy discourse on their waywardness - their filthy doings - and their iniquities -- Neither do I give discourse on their virtues -- I say - I come that they might be prepared for the Greater part. Wherein have they profited by their great and lengthy discourses? - Have they prepared themself? - Are they free from their legirons which bind them? -- Have they the mind which is in Me? -- Have they prepared themself to enter into the Holy of Holies? Nay Mine child - they have not learned the meaning of "preparation" - They have become puffed up. They have bound themself in -- They have wrapt themself about with their own bounds -- Wherein can they be reached?

I say they are BIGOTS - and hypocrites! - They are but a stench in Our nostrils -- I say they shall bow down and worship the LORD GOD of HOSTS - and love one another.

They shall bind up the wounds of their slaves - and the enemy -- And they shall cleanse out the privies which they have filled to overflowing ---

I say - the hypocrites and bigots shall find no resting place until they have first cleaned themself of all their hypocrisy - and falsehood!

So be it I shall speak again on that subject---

I Am come that there be Light -- Be ye blest of Me and by Me ---

I AM Sanat Kumara

Recorded by Sister Thedra of the Emerald Cross

I Would That Ye Know the Power of the Word

Beloved Ones -- I speak unto thee this day as One illumined of Mine Father -- So be it I Know whereof I speak -- For it is no accident that We come to know the power of the Word by which We are illumined - It is by the Power of the Word -- And the Word is Power -- And pure is its Essence -- And no man can pilfer that power or make of it a plaything -- For _it_ is that which he can not defile or pilfer ---

I say: Man can not defile the Power - that which is the Word spoken from out the Mouth of the Mighty Father Which is the Source of Our Being --- I say unto thee that it is not by accident that We come to Know the Power of the Spoken Word -- The Power is spoken as the First Fiat: "Let There Be" and it BECAME -- And therein is Power! I would that you come to Know this Power of which I speak -- Let it Be- for I have decreed it So ---

So be it I shall speak again and again -- I bless thee with Mine Being---

So be it I AM -

Sananda

Recorded by Sister Thedra of the Emerald Cross

Sananda's Blessing

Beloved Ones -- With Mine own hand thou hast been blest - For I have placed upon thine head Mine hand - and pronounced the Word -- And it is now come that ye shall remember that which I have said unto thee. Ye shall remember thine Being - and ye shall Know that thou are One with Me -- and that thou art not of the Earth - as of common clay ---

I tell thee - thou hast not come into the fullness of thine inheritance.

Yet it is not spent - it awaits thee -- It is thine by Divine inheritance. All thine ways are not sufficient unto thine maturing -- It is given unto Me that I Am the Lord thy God - sent that ye might be brot to the age of maturity -- Therefore I have given of Mineself that it be So ---

So be it I proffer thee Mine hand - and I say unto thee - accept it in the Name of the Father which hast sent Us forth as the First Born -- And at no time shall He turn Us aside - So be it I speak unto thee this hour - that ye be blest ---

Hear ye Me - and Know ye that I AM with thee--

I AM -

Sananda

Recorded by Sister Thedra of the Emerald Cross

THE MIGHTY SON KNOWN AS SANANDA

Behold the Lord thy God -- See the hand move - and know ye that He is the Host of Hosts -- I say unto thee - Behold the Lord thy God and see that which shall be done -- For there shall be Great things accomplished this day -- And nothing shall stay the Power of God - which is established in the Host. I say the Host has the Power -- It is invested within Him -- For He has been given the Power by the Father which has brot Him forth ---

So be it that He - the Mighty Son known as Sananda shall be unto the Father His hand made flesh -- Made manifest upon the Earth as One of flesh - that flesh might be lifted up.-

I Say: "That Flesh Might Be Lifted Up"---

So shall it Be -- For when He comes into the radius of man - man partakes of HIS RADIENCE -- So shall the Earth too - be blest that HE sets foot upon Her soil ---

Now it is said - that ye shall touch the hem of His Garment it is so and ye shall be blest indeed -- For He shall walk amongst thee and bless thee as none other ---

It is not necessary that He bear His Wounds - that ye put thine fingers therein -- This is to be no more -- It is finished/done with - and shall be no more! - Ask not such proof -- For the false one can show the signs and wonders - that he deceive thee -- Ye shall know the Mighty Son of God, known unto <u>Us</u> as Sananda (The Host) - as the Lord God of Hosts -- This One is the One sent of the Father that the Word be made manifest. That there be established upon the Earth a

New Order -- And that the WORD be made clear unto them which seek Light ---

Let them which seek signs and wonders have them -- Yet I say the false one can give unto them that which shall mystify them - and hold them bound – They shall run after him and worship at his shrine in remembrance of his magic.

I say unto thee - be ye no part of his magic -- Seek not after strange and magic things - strange phenomena - and the things which are new unto thee ---

I say: These things of Spirit are not new -- They are no part of magic-- They are foretold long ago - and need no repeating herein -I say unto thee free thineself of thine preconceived opinions and ideas -- Cast aside thine legirons Seek ye Truth - Light - and obey ye the law - And no man can turn thee aside -- I Am come that ye might be delivered of all thine bondage - all that which holds thee bound -- Let it profit thee that I have spoken unto thee thusly -- For it behooves Me to add Mine Part this day - that it Be -- That ye too might come into the fullness of thine estate ---

I bless the with Mine Presence --

For this have I come --

I AM - Maheru -

Recorded by Sister Thedra of the Emerald Cross

Spirit is Not a Thing

Beloved Ones -- I say unto thee this day -- Spirit is not bound, it is free. It is not a "Thing" - It is the Substance out of which All things are come. It is that which animates the <u>pore</u> -- Let not thine pore represent the "Whole" - for the pore is but a poor part of thine self.

It is with great concern that We see them entrapt within the "poor part" -- They give unto the "pore" power -- They <u>think</u> themself to be the <u>pore</u> -- It is not so! I tell thee - the pore is but the vehicle of "Spirit" and Spirit is limitless ---

I speak of <u>this</u> Substance out of which manifestation comes - as "Spirit"-- While thou hast used that term - thou canst best understand it. Therefore I shall use it for thine sake -- I tell thee thou <u>art</u> <u>not</u> the pore -- And the pore shall <u>not</u> bind thee -- I Am come that ye be "free" Know ye thine freedom - accept it - for it is the Reality of thine BEING.

See ye the hand of God move -- Know ye that it moveth - And be ye as ones blest thereby -- I say be ye as ones blest to see the hand of God move -- I Am sent that it be so -- So let it be ---

I AM Sananda

Recorded by Sister Thedra of the Emerald Cross

Self Analysis -- The Cup

Sori Sori -- Hast not thine feet been slow to go in the Way in which I lead? Hast thine tongue been swift to speak that which I speak? Hast thine eyes beheld the Glory of the Lord? Hast thou remembered the sayings of the Lord thy God? Hast thou been true unto thineself - and hast thou attained thine Victory? ---

I ask of thee - hast thou prepared thineself that ye might enter into the Holy of Holies -- Into the Place wherein ALL things are Known?

Let it be understood - that thine own preparation is the Greatest concern -- Wait not for another -- Pass not the cup until thou hast drunken thereof - and it shall be for thine own good that ye drink deeply thereof ---

Hast it not been said: "First drink of the cup then pass it unto thine Brother" -- Should he refuse it - condemn him not!

For he hast not as yet the will to partake of Mine Board.

While I say unto thee - all which do drink of Mine Cup shall thirst no more -- So be it I too have drunken of the Cup before I give it unto thee-- I have found it "Sweet" indeed - and I bid thee drink! DRINK DEEPLY! And be ye satisfied For this have I proffered it unto thee -- I give unto thee No Strange Concoctions - which I have conjured up -- I have been given the Cup of Mine Father which hast sent Me -- And I KNOW it to be Sweet -- Therefore I bid thee Drink and be refreshed.

While it is given unto thee to taste of many Waters - many stagnant and filthy -- I bring unto thee "Water" ye know not of -- For this reason I speak unto thee thusly ---

I say unto thee which have a mind to comprehend that which I say "I Bring Waters ye Know not of" -- Therefore I speak with the voice of Mine Father which hast sent Me -- DRINK ye of the cup which I proffer thee -- I AM the ONE sent that ye might have that which hast been kept for thee -- And it is because I have drunken of it that I know it to be the <u>Water</u> <u>of</u> <u>Eternal</u> <u>Life</u> ---

Let thine eyes be opened that ye might see-- Let thine feet be swift to follow where I lead thee--

Let thine mind be the mind which is in ME --

Let thine heart rejoice forevermore ---

So Be It I AM - Sananda

Recorded by Sister Thedra of the Emerald Cross

The Gift of Sight

Sori Sori Behold this day the Glory of the Lord -- I say unto thee - See ye that which shall be done -- For the time is come when ye shall stand face to face with Him - and ye shall Know Him ---

Be ye as ones prepared - for it is nigh time when He shall give unto thee the Gift of Sight - and ye shall behold Him in ALL HIS GLORY!

I speak unto thee this day - that ye be blest of Me and by Me -- Accept Mine blessing in the Name of Mine Father which hast sent Me. So be it I Am Come that ye might come to know Him as I Know Him.

Wherein is it said that "As ye receive ME - ye receive the Father". So be it - as ye will it---

Let this day bring forth Great Light - Great Joy - and be ye blest thereby -- Stand ye steadfast - and I shall reveal many things unto thee. So be it and Selah ---

I AM - Sananda

Sanandas Benediction

Behold Me the Lord thy God -- Se ye that which I shall do!- Know ye that I AM the Lord thy God - and bless ye this day.- Keep thine lamp trimmed - and I shall fill it to overflowing.

Harken ye unto Mine Word and Know ye that I shall Keep Mine Covenant with thee -- Be ye as ones blest this day-- Wait upon Me - and I shall be unto thee Servant - Let thine Light so shine that All might see it - and be drawn unto it ---

Rest ye in the Knowing that I AM with thee-- Be ye as Mine hand, Mine foot - and go ye where I send thee -- Do ye that which I give unto thee to do - and abide in Me - and I shall abide in thee---

I AM - Sananda

Recorded by Sister Thedra of the Emerald Cross

Who are They?

Sanat Kumara

Beloved of Mine Being - Be ye blest of Me and by Me - For this do I speak unto thee this day -- It is Mine part to give unto thee this Word that they might know that which I say unto thee ---

I speak unto thee that they might have this Mine Word -- Now let it be recorded thusly:- I am the One sent that these Words be recorded as they are spoken -- So let it be ---

There are Ones Known as the Counselors - as the "Great Host" - the Council - and as the Ones known as the "Sibors" I say unto thee - These are not divided - against themself -- Yet they are made up of a Goodly Company - and of an Order Known as the Brotherhood of Man under the Fatherhood of God the Father --

The <u>Cause</u> of Our Being -- These are of the Mighty Eloheim - the Council of Seven Lights - the Seven Eloheim - and the Head of the Host - which is Our Blessed and Benevolent Brother Sananda -- I say He is the Host of Hosts -- It is for this that We Bow unto Him - that We give unto Him the due Honor which is His --

He is the Head of the Galactic Confederacy - and the Head of the Mighty Council I tell thee that the Name Sananda is not new to Us of the Mighty Council -- Yet it hast been revealed unto thee <u>first</u> - within the Western World -- For it wast from the beginning so designed - that ye should bring forth this NAME - this <u>News</u> of <u>His</u> <u>Return</u> unto the world of men -- I say it is by Divine Intent that it is so that it was foreknown that it be so.

So be it that this shall be recorded for all time - and none shall foreswear Mine Word unto thee -- For I say it is given unto Me to <u>Know</u> that which <u>goes</u> <u>on</u> in the world of men. I say unto thee - I ask no man for his word - that Mine be validated. I Know whereof I speak - and I am not deceived by their plunderings-- So be it that I Am One of the Council - and I Am Justified by Mine Father - which hast sent Me -- So be it that I shall speak again of this subject---

I AM thine Elder Brother

Sanat Kumara

Recorded by Sister Thedra of the Emerald Cross

Blessed are They

Blessed art Thou - For ye shall see Me face to face --

    Blessed art they which seek Me out - for I shall

    reveal Mineself unto them ---

    Blessed art they which wait upon Me - for I shall

    show Mine face unto them –

    Blessed art they which Keep the Law - for they shall

    be delivered out of bondage --

    Blessed art they which walk with Me - for they

    shall Know Me --

    Blessed art they which Know Me - for they shall

Know the Father Which hast sent Me --

Blessed art they which Know the Father - for they

shall be as One with Him --

Blessed art they which Are One with Him - for they

Shall abide with Him forever More --

So be it - I AM Come that ye be delivered out --

Let it Be -- For this I have

Revealed Minself unto thee

I AM

Sananda

Recorded by Sister Thedra of the Emerald Cross

He is Come That Ye Be Lifted Up

Be ye as Ones Lifted Up -- Be ye as Ones - Come Alive!

Be ye as Ones prepared to Behold the Glory of the Lord.

For I say unto thee - I the Lord thy God shall go forth declaring openly that I AM COME ---

I AM COME -

I AM COME that they be delivered up ---

Yet t<u>hey</u> shall have the mind to follow where I lead them for they shall follow of their own Will -- And for that hast been given the Will endowed unto them of the Father which hast Sent Me --

I say: Behold the Glory of the Lord - for He is Risen! He is COME that ye be Lifted Up ---

Let thine heart rejoice that it is <u>Now</u> come that All the Land shall be made to rejoice --

For there shall come forth One which shall bless the L<u>an</u>d - and it shall be purged and purified - and No Longer shall the traitors and the laggards pollute Her - for She hast carried them on Her back for long and they shall be Removed - and She too shall be delivered out of bondage -- I say - Behold the Work which I shall do!

I Am Come that there shall be Light - Which shall bring forth Great Change ---

And Change there Shall be ---

Now ye shall take Mine Word unto thine Self - and look not for Signs and Wonders - for I say unto thee -- I AM COME -- I AM COME.

Behold the Glory of The Lord --

He is Come --

So be it - I AM HE --

The Lord thy God --

Sent of Mine Father –

Solen Aum Solen

Recorded by Sister Thedra of the Emerald Cross

Thine Origin - Solen Aum Solen

Beloved Ones -- I speak unto them which are prepared to receive Mine Word -- I tell thee for a surety - that ye shall not defile the Name of Solen Aum Solen - The <u>Cause</u> of thine Being ---

It is the Most Sacred Name thou canst breathe forth -- I tell thee it is thine Being -- None other hast fashioned thee -- It is by His Grace that thou hast Life - and Being -- Thou hast <u>not</u> come up from the dust! Thou hast not come from out of the void of thine own volition -- Thou art not sufficient unto thine self -- Thou art not the poor part of clay (the pore). Thou art Divine in thine Origin - and it behooves ME to speak unto thee of that Origin ---

While thou hast not as yet remembered it - thou shall come to remember it -- Thou shall indeed return unto thine SOURCE - and then ye shall <u>Know</u> full well - that Thou hast returned unto thine Abiding Place -- So be it that Thou hast but to see the Light of the Father - which hast IMAGED THEE PERFECT -- While it is given unto thee to walk in flesh - as ones bound by flesh - I say unto thee - <u>hold</u> <u>ye</u> <u>no</u> <u>illusion</u> for flesh is flesh - and subject unto its laws - the laws of Earth -- I speak unto thee as One which Knows whereof I speak -- I say: - Flesh is bound by the law of Earth it is of the Earth - and comes under such law -- Now too I say: - Ye shall obey the law which I set forth - which is for thine own freedom - brot forth from the beginning - and given unto thee from the beginning --

Recorded that ye might Know that Thou art not of Earth - that Thou Art Divine - that thou hast a fortune willed unto thee of the "Father" - Solen Aum Solen -- So be ye as ones obedient unto it -- Walk ye in the WAY set before thee - and ye shall transcend the law of flesh -- Arise as on wings - and be free from such law as binds thee -- So be it that I have spoken much of the law of gravitation and the attraction of the Moon -- I shall again speak of it -- Be ye as ones which hear that which I say unto thee ---

I Am Come that ye be free -- So be it as ye will it ---

I AM - Sananda

Recorded by Sister Thedra of the Emerald Cross

Great Onrush of Spirit

Soran -- Beloved -- I bring forth this day a part designed for the Children of Earth - which are prepared to receive it -- It is a simple one in the manner in which they might comprehend -- For this is it simple.

Let it be said that there shall be a Great and Mighty Onrush of Spirit. It shall be a Great Awakening - - And the ones which have been given shall have more -- I say - them which have received shall receive more -- For them which have not - shall not receive - for these are the ones which have <u>not</u> accepted that which hast been proffered them -- These are the ones which have not accepted US of the Higher Council and that which We have proffered unto them -- These shall be found wanting -- So be it and Selah ---

While it is not yet come that they Know the fullness of the Plan, it is apparent that they are lacking within themself -- They are not sufficient unto themself -- They which turn from the Light - seeking for What? - in strange places - are the ones which shall be caught up short These shall be as ones crying unto their UNKNOWN GOD for help -- Their cries shall be heard thruout the land - and they shall not be answered -- For it is said: "Ye shall first prepare thineself - for to receive of Us and by Us of the Mighty Host - The Mighty Council -- Let it be said that when they do deny the Word - they deny the Host -- Too - it is said: "They which are prepared shall receive as they are prepared --

So it shall be - for it is the law -- It is the Law which is born out of Truth and Justice that We bring -- While they Call themself Christ-ians or any other name which they give unto themself - it is given unto Us of the Mighty Council to Know them - that which they do - that which they shall do -- Too - We Know their capacity for hatred for Love - for work - for sleep. For it is by their light that We Know them -- We are not deceived by their words (their prayers) -- They are not the strangers unto Us that We are unto them ---

It is Mine part to proffer Mine hand unto ALL -- Let them which are prepared - take it and be forever blest ---

I AM One of the Council - One of the EL-O-Heim -

Recorded by Sister Thedra of the Emerald Cross

Easter

Sori Sori - Hasten Ye to say unto them in Mine Name - that there are none which have donned the FINE RAIMENT* which is of Light Substance - deceived by their display of finery - their bouquets their fine clothes - and showy parties wherein they display them! -- I say they do make a <u>mockery</u> of Mine Name -- They are worse than PAGANS -- They are wont to bring themself unto Me - as a living sacrifice -- They are wont to bring themself as a LIVING SACRIFICE! I say they are not prepared to follow where I lead them-- They are hypocrites and adulterers!! ---

I speak out against them - for they are not that which they profess to be- and I Know them -- They display their ignorance of Me - and of Mine Nature -- THEY KNOW ME NOT - and I say unto them - "BE YE AS ONES PREPARED TO RECEIVE ME - AND OF ME"-- Yet they have <u>not</u> prepared themself by their display of fancy garments and gaudy gadgets -- Let it be said - they are hypocrites - and know Me not. I am come that they might have LIGHT -- So be it they have bound themself to their tradition - their former darkness and they ask not for Light -- They ask for pageantry - and for great wealth of display -- I say unto them: Go feed the hungry --

Go give unto the needy -- Go give of thine energy unto the lame - halt - the blind - sick and frail of spirit -- Comfort the dying - and bury the dead!! -- Give of thineself and expose not thine ignorance of Me/the Law/ and thine Unknowing -- Ask of the Father - LIGHT - and it shall not be denied thee -- Seek the LIGHT with thine WHOLE Heart - and it shall be revealed unto thee ---

I AM COME that it Be So -- Let it be as ye will it ---

I AM Sananda

The Lord thy God

Recorded by Sister Thedra of the Emerald Cross

* Those who have traveled The Royal Road -

Sarah - "Being -- The Fullness Thereof"

Sarah Speaking -- Beloved Children --Mine arms encompass thee - Mine hand enfolds thee -- Thine life is Mine Life --Thou art the Children of Mine own BEING -- Thou art the ones which I have brot forth - thou art Not separate from ME.

When it is said thou art Mine hands - Mine feet - it is so. Thou art the manifestation of Mine Self - in the world of manifestation - and thou art the manifestation ---

While it is given unto Me to be the "Whole" - the ALL - thou art part of the 'Whole" - the part which thou callest "Self" -- Yet it is given unto thee to be but a fragment of the "Whole" - the Whole being the Complete and the ALL -- Now I say unto thee - thou Art One with Me the Whole - the ALL - and thou shall come to Know thineself to Be - Thou shall Come to Know that thou art not but a fragment - but the fullness of ME ---

Thou shall come into the FULLNESS of thine BEING -- Then ye shall know that which I have kept for thee -- Then ye shall See and Know as I Know -- And then ye shall do that which I do - and be as

One with Me -- So be it that I have kept thee for t<u>h</u>is d<u>a</u>y -- Be ye as One and Love ye One Another - and Know ye that thou art not separate from Me - for I Am the Life - the Manifestation - the <u>Fullness</u> of thine BEING --

So be it - I AM the Everness

I AM thine Mother Eternal

> **Recorded by Sister Thedra of the Emerald Cross**

The Hidden Part

This is Mine time -- And I shall speak unto thee of the part which is hidden from the unjust and the imprudent -- These are the ones which turn their face from ME - that they might <u>not</u> see -- Now hear that which I say unto them -- These are the ones which have given unto themself credit for being W<u>ise</u> -- These are the ones which have given unto man the credit for being Great - and they see not that which is hidden from them ---

Now I would say unto them: Be ye as ones which have betrayed thine own self -- Know ye from whence thou came? Know ye whither thou goest? -- And when it is given unto thee to Know these things - THEN ye might call thineself WISE ---

So be it I come that there be Light -- Yet I give unto thee that which thou art prepared to receive -- While thou hast not asked of Me - I await thine call -- Yet ye shall not mock Me for I am not deceived -- I am not short-sighted -- I see and Know thine motives -and feign not fidelity - thou hypocrite!!

Mighty is the WORD and Great the POWER thereof -- And it behooves Me to say unto thee - every W<u>or</u>d shall be accounted for -Let no word pass thine lips which would be unto thee thine undoing! - Defile not thine word with the power of the dark one -- It is given unto the unknowing ones to defile themself with vain speech - with profanity/obscenity and with the language of the hypocrite - that which they pilfer, their vain sayings - and their poor part of knowing For they but poll-parrot their sayings - their platitudes for their own sake - Wherein hast it profited them?

Now let it be said: that every word shall be accounted for. And at no time shall ye be as ones exempt from the law - for the law is exact - and is no favorite of persons ---

The word is a creating force - and it is conditioned by the word which goes out from thine mouth -- It shall return unto thee - either for weal or woe ---

Now it behooves Me to say that the word is the power -- And at no time shall ye misuse the power -- So be it ye shall ponder well these Mine sayings -- Waste not thine energy - for it is sacred -- It is thine for thine own use -- Use it wisely and feign not righteousness Let thine lips not belie thine heart -- I Am He which Knows the LAW - and I say unto thee be ye as ones intent on the G<u>reater</u> P<u>ar</u>t Be ye not frivolous or flippant -- And heed the Word Spoken in All Love - and for this is it given unto thee - that they might Know - that they might be as ones prepared to receive Me and of Me –

So be it and Selah -- Behold Me - the Lord

thy God -- I AM Sananda

> **Recorded by Sister Thedra of the Emerald Cross**

Wherein Hast Thou Been Schooled?

Wherein has thou been schooled that thou canst deny the Word of the LORD?

Wherein hast thou dwelt that ye have seen the Glory of the LORD?

Wherein hast thou been as ones ILLUMINATED?

Wherein hast thou GIVEN of thineself that others be comforted that others be freed from bondage?

These things I would ask of thee - as I now speak unto the ones which doth cry out for help ---

I would ask of them many things - Yet I say unto them - "Blessed are the Ones which ask for Light" -- Yet they shall seek w<u>ithin</u> the Light. They shall seek with their Whole BEING - and it shall not be part time - or by word of mouth They shall ask of the Father - the S<u>ource</u> of their BEING - for Light -- Yet they seek within the realm of men -- They deny that which I say unto them-- They deny the WORD which I give unto them -- Yet they ask of "men" their opinions - their blessing and their assistance -- They turn unto the deadly stimulants for assistance - yet they have not accepted ME - neither the Word which I bring ---

I say - to deny the Word which I bring - is to deny ME - for Mine Word is SACRED -- And it is for this that I give it unto thee -- I say I give not a stone for BREAD --- I give unto thee that which would profit thee---

It is said that there is much sameness within the "WORD"-- Wherein hast it been changed? - Wherein have I betrayed Mineself? I say unto them: I Am come that there be Light! -- --

It shall be seen - and it shall be for the reason that I AM COME!! For this shall it be seen.

Let it be said that I Come - Not for to deliver Great and Learned Speeches - that they have some new and strange doctrine. I Come that they might Know the LAW- that they might prepare themself for the Greater Part - their ETERNAL FREEDOM - that they might enter into the Holy of Holies wherein I Abide ---

So be it they have not heard that which I say unto them -- They are as ones yet rebelling against ME - against MINE WORD -- Yet they cry out for Peace - for surcease from their WOES --- These are the ones which raise their voice against ME - and Mine Servants --

I say unto them "Behold ME, Behold Mine Servant and See that which I shall do" that which Mine Servants shall do -- For they shall do a MIGHTY WORK - and it shall be GOOD -- So I say unto thee WATCH! - LOOK! - LISTEN! - SEE! - and KNOW! -- And be ye as ones prepared to go where I lead thee ---

So be it that I the Lord thy God Am Sent that Ye be Free. So let it be --- I AM Sananda -

Son of the Father Solen Aum Solen

Recorded by Sister Thedra of the Emerald Cross

Sananda's Benediction

Beloved Ones -- This day I would say unto thee - Be ye blest of Mine Presence - of Mine Power - Mine Word -- And let it be that I Am Come that ye be blest. -- For this have I placed Mine hand upon thee-- Be ye as ones prepared for thine New Part - and I shall pronounce the Word which shall bless thee and the Work of thine hands -- For it shall be Mine Work - that which I shall give unto thee to do -- And it shall be Well with thee -- So be it and Selah--

Fortune unto thineself the Great Joy of serving Me - that Others be blest of Me - thru thee -- For this have I called thee, Mine Servants I say unto thee - thou art "Mine Servants" - and Great shall be thine reward. Too - I say ye shall not falter - neither shall ye fail -- Be ye alert - be ye not tempted for I the Lord thy God know the pitfalls. I too know the weakness of flesh -- Be ye as ones which have had Mine hand upon thee - and Know ye that I Am Come that ye be blest.

So shall it BE --

I AM -

Sananda

Recorded by Sister Thedra of the Emerald Cross

Sananda's Benediction

Sori Sori - Behold the Glory of the Lord and rejoice that this day is come! Behold that which shall be done this day - and Know ye that it is the day for which thou hast waited -- LONG hast thou awaited this day - when ye might See the GLORY of The Lord -- I say - BEHOLD THE GLORY OF THE LORD THY GOD -- So be it ye shall Rejoice and be Glad!

I say unto thee - WALK YE AS SONS OF GOD - and REJOICE, For I AM COME that IT BE SO ---

So let it Be ---

I have spoken and thou hast heard ME -

So be it Ye shall be

Blest of Me and by

ME -- I AM - Sananda

Recorded by Sister Thedra of the Emerald Cross

Soran - Representing the Great Council

Soran - Beloved -- On this day - at this time - it is given unto Me to give unto thee this WORD -- And it shall be thine part to give it unto them which doth call themself Servants of God. It shall be for their own sake that it shall go forth - and it shall bless them which doth receive it.

Wherein hast it been said that "The Way is Opened for them which Choose to follow in the Way set before them - thru and by the Great Council" - which I represent herein ---

Now it shall be recorded thusly: It is the Plan which I represent that permits Me to speak at this time -- For I Come thru the Mighty Council, the Great Council - which is A<u>bov</u>e a<u>n</u>d O<u>v</u>er A<u>ll</u> Ot<u>her</u>s.

I come as One representing the Law - the Order of the Sibors - the Great and Glorious Company - Which is called the "WHITE STAR" - It is thru <u>This</u> <u>Order</u> that thou hast been prepared to receive this Word any and ALL communication of the Higher Order ---

While it is said - and rightfully so - that there are ones which doth come as imposters - as imitators - and as the traitors - I say they are n<u>ot</u> of t<u>his</u> ORDER - of which I come.

There are ones which pilfer and adulterate - and misuse that which is given thru this Order-- Yet they alone are responsible for that which <u>they</u> do - Be ye no part of their misused energy -- Let it be established that I have appointed thee Mine Spokesman - and I have set aside Mine Voice - that ye might speak for Me concerning these things ---

It is for this that thou hast been called out from amongst them -- I have gathered thee in - and I have Sibored thee - that ye might be so prepared -- So be it that I shall speak for the Board at this time.

When it is given unto one to answer the call to Service it is his duty to take a certain Oath and to stand ready to serve any place/anywhere/any time without question. This he hast sworn to do: uphold his oath of Justice/Service/Loyalty unto the laws of his land. So be it the law -- When he breaks that oath - he is indeed a traitor unto himself- unto his trust -- He becomes an "Outcast". So it is with the "Great Council" which I represent ---

When one is called - and he answers that call - and presents himself as a C<u>andidate</u> - he is given the law - the way is shown him. He is expected to uphold the law - and justify himself - and walk in the way shown him -- He is carefully guarded and guided - He is given his own <u>Free</u> <u>Will,</u> it is never trespassed upon-- He has at all times his <u>Free</u> <u>Will</u>. He either brings unto the Altar himself as a LIVING SACRIFICE - that he be an example of the Candidate - or he turns aside as "Unfit Timber". He has that way to choose - He hast been called - and he hast refused to prepare himself. This is his trial and error -- It is said that they are not prepared.

They are as the u<u>nripene</u>d seed -- They have not the strength of Character - therefore the "Initiate" does not fo<u>rc</u>h upon him <u>his</u> part - for he is frail of spirit - and can not carry the burden of the Initiate-- He simply does not have the capacity or the strength - neither the W<u>ill</u> to be strengthened.

Now it is come when there shall be a Great On-rush of Spirit - and a Great Surge of Light shall go forth - and it shall stir them - they shall fall - they shall raise up - they shall cry, they shall laugh - they shall sing glad songs and they shall dance -- They shall express that which they feel - yet this is not sufficient!

They shall render up themself as a <u>Living</u> <u>S</u>acrifice - that the Father might Glorify Himself in them -- They shall praise Him - and He shall justify them - for He is The Father which hast sent them forth ---

Now let it be understood that there are ones amongst them which are of the nether world -- And these are the soulless ones - which are not capable of Eternal Life -- I say these are of the prince of darkness. These are animated - and these are the ones which shall be disarmed and cast out ---

For they shall hold power no longer -- This is the time long spoken of -- For this is the time which is recorded within thine books of learning -- When they shall <u>run riot</u> - overrun the Earth - and blood shall flow in the streets -- It is recorded that there shall become such condition as ye now see about thee -- And yet they count themself prophets of forecoming events -- And set themself up as priests - declaring it is <u>afar off</u> --

Mine Children - I say unto thee - THIS IS THE DAY - This is the times which hast been prophesied long ago -- And at no time hast the world seen such conflict -- Let it be said that the Initiate shall be no part of their onslaught -- Their own way hast been theirs for the choosing - So be it that I have spoken - that it might be made clear unto the Candidate that <u>He</u> is responsible for himself - for his actions - and the result thereof -- <u>He</u> shall blame no other for his own weakness.-

While I shall speak of the Initiates part at a later hour - I say that the Candidate shall hear that which I say - and obey the laws given unto him -- He shall follow in the way shown him -- So be it I shall speak again this day --- Soran

Beloved -- Ye shall again take up thine pen and record that which I say unto the Initiate -- For it is the way of the Initiate - which is the Greatest concern unto this Company -- For it is the way of the Initiate that We place before thee ---

It is the Way of the Initiate that We Go - that All shall follow which are of the mind to attain ---

Wherein is it said that the Way of the Initiate is the Way of attainment -- For it is the Initiate which does attain unto the Heights.

Now it is given unto Me to be One of the Host - and at no time are We unmindful of the Candidate -- For We extend unto them Our hand in fellowship - in love and compassion - Yet he has the will to take it or leave it-- We are not wont to cast any shadows upon him. We are not of a mind to bring him without his preparation -- For it is not possible. It is the Way of the Initiate to speak - when it is so indicated that he should and he shall Know when it is so indicated.

He is N<u>o</u>t given unto vain boasting - or to flattery -- He is <u>At All Times</u> honest - humble - and a man amongst men -- He walks upright, honorable in ALL his dealings. He flaunts not himself before men. He sits not upon the seat of judgement as one pronouncing judgement of his brethren. I say he has the Love of God within himself - for he hast established Peace within himself -- So be it that it hast been said before, yet it shall be said again and again that the Initiate hast <u>attaine</u>d thru his preparation thru and by obedience - and a<u>pplicatio</u>n unto it.

Let it be recorded that none other can attain for him -- None other can bring him -- He is responsible for himself -- For there is no such law as Vicarious Atonement -- Let this be understood - and Great shall be the day when they learn this law of Self-Preparation -- I shall speak again of preparation --- I AM - Soran

This shall be added unto the other part for the Initiate -- The Initiate shall at All times be prepared to go where called or where sent -- He shall stand ready to serve in any capacity so indicated -- He shall not be deceived - for that is the part of wisdom - to Know wherein he shall serve - to the Glory of Our Father-- So be it that he shall KNOW the True from the false -- He shall be quick to respond to the call of the Council and he shall serve with the Greatest Joy. He shall be quick to give of himself unto the Candidate - yet he shall not tr<u>espa</u>ss upon his f<u>re</u>e w<u>il</u>l -- He shall be as an "Older Brother" unto the Younger -- And when it is expedient - he shall say that which is wise and gainly -- He shall not betray himself - or show his hand unto the unjust or the <u>Bigot</u> -- He shall be at all times the Ambassador - which represents the Council of Light --

He shall be the One to set before the lesser the signpost that they might find their way -- Let it be said that he shall not allow the laggards to ride his back -- He shall not be subservient unto them -- He grovels not for a pittance He asks no favors -- He fortunes unto himself the service which is his reward -- He beholds no evil in his fellowman - He sees them as the unripened fruit-- He Knows them for that which they are - and he gives no quarter -- Neither does he ask anything of any man - he bargains not -- He is not frustrated by the going and coming of man -- He is not wont to be the leader of men-- He is not wont to express his wisdom unto them - that they might marvel at his great and profound knowledge -- He is at All times humble of spirit - and gentle of the manner ---

(Wait for the next part)

While it is now come what ye have prepared thineself to receive this part - let it be recorded that they might have it - and for that do I give it unto thee ---

When it is so indicated that the Candidate be at any place he shall immediately go forth - and be as the Candidate -- He shall conduct himself becomingly - and listen unto that which is said unto him -- He shall speak when spoken to - without the flippancy which is the fortune of the unknowing ones -- He shall be serious in his manner of speech - and Know that which he is about -- He shall ask no favors, neither shall he run hither and yon - looking for the easy path.

He shall be as the One which is responsible unto himself for his lot. He shall have no part in the frivolity of the foolish -- He shall bring himself as a Living Sacrifice - a Living Example - and be as One Noble of thot - peaceful - loving and gentle of manner -- He shall be considerate of the one which hast been unto him Sibor - unto him the shield and buckler -- He shall be as the shield unto the lesser ones -- He shall count his blessings - and find no fault with his <u>Elders,</u> the Ones which have sponsored him ---

I say - this is the part which I have given unto thee for the Candidate. So be it - it shall profit him to heed that which I have said. So be it ye shall be blest of Me and by Me ---

I AM - Soran

Recorded by Sister Thedra of the Emerald Cross

Nothing Is Hidden

Soran

Soran -- Be ye as ones trustworthy - and ye shall be given the "Greater Part" -- It is said: "Be ye trustworthy and the Great and Grand Assembly shall take note of thee" ---

While many have pro<u>fesse</u>d <u>t</u>he W<u>or</u>d - they heed not the law.

It is said: They shall be tried and found trustworthy - and then they shall be given as they are prepared to receive -- So be it the <u>Law.</u>

Now it is come when many shall be gathered together in one body and they shall be liken unto the 'traitors' -- They shall prepare a part for the people - and they shall call it "Good" - yet it shall be their own - and in no way shall it be <u>Good</u> -- It shall be on their own terms - and designed to hold fast their subjects -- It shall be so designed - for this is not a new thing -- It is not <u>new</u> to them - and WE of the Higher Realm have seen them coming and going - making way for their v<u>ictim</u>s - which they are wont to hold bound ---

Now it is given unto Me to say - they shall be as ones bound by that which they choose to bring forth -- Yet they shall have no power over My People- that they be bound -- Wherein is it said "they shall drink their own bitter cup" -- So shall it be ---

Now I say unto thee: "Be ye as ones prepared for the fullness of the Plan" - and at no time be ye caught up in their nefarious plan -- Stand ye steadfast -- Know ye that thou art not alone ---

I say there are many which doth stand by to assist -- At no time shall they forsake thee -- Let it be said - that they are not of a mind to betray themself -- They are sent of God the Father - that He might be <u>glorifie</u>d upon the Earth - and that His Kingdom be e<u>stablishe</u>d. So shall it be ---

Let it be said that the Way is now open - that ye be delivered out. See it! Walk ye therein and be ye forever blest for this have We entered into thine world - that ye be lifted up ---

I AM - Soran

Recorded by Sister Thedra of the Emerald Cross

Mission Statement

Give the truth to the world. Let it be received where it will. Many will read the messages. Some will accept the truth, others will read through curiosity, a few will ridicule. Yet to all is the truth given, and to all remains the power of choice.

The hope of the world in these times is in spiritualizing all forms of activity---promoting understanding through love and service. These must be the watchwords if the world is to come into lasting peace. We are trying to influence a world that is going astray and could cause undreamed of suffering. We are trying to overcome the thought of materialists and to bring a spiritual outlook into the earthly life. We need the help of all on earth who can think in spiritual terms. The great battle to be fought now is between the spiritual and the material, between idealism and carnalism. You can help by spreading the word---we are asking that you help because the battle may be long and the victory far away.

Halls of Light is not allied with any sect, denomination, political entity, organization, neither endorses nor opposes any cause. There are no dues for membership. Halls of Light is self-supporting through its own voluntary contributions. Halls of Light has but one purpose: to help through encouragement and understanding...

To contact the publishers or to obtain copies of our other books, please contact us at email: goldtown11@gmail.com

Sananda's Appearance

Be ye as one which hast heard Mine Voice and responded unto it - for I speak that ye hear, and I say that which is wise and prudent.

Let it be known that 1, the Lord thy God hast spoken and bear ye witness of Me, for I have made manifest Mineself that ye might know Me - and for this wast these manifestations made.

I say that I have made Mineself manifest that ye might see Me with thine mortal eyes; that ye might bear witness of Me. Yet thine companions saw and believed not; neither did they hear, for they were selfish and unprepared - yet, did I deny them?

I say; I came that they which would might see and hear. I went and came again unto Mine own. So be it that I have found; I have given unto the found that they which know not might know; that they might come to know as thou knowest.

Yet, how many hast turned from Me and persecuted thee for Mine Word. It is said, "Woe unto them which persecute Mine servants." is it not the law which they set into motion?

Yea Mine beloved, I say they bring about their own downfall. So be it that I am a compassionate one, and I would that they know what they do. So be it they shall learn well their lessons. So let it be, for this is the mercy of God, the One which hast sent Me.

So be it. I AM The Wayshower, the Lord thy God

I AM Sananda

About the Late Sister Thedra

Since the later part of the last Century, the *Kumara* wisdom has begun to reemerge into the world. This process began with the late Sister Thedra, whom Jesus Christ appeared physically to while on her deathbed and spontaneously healed her of cancer while she was in the Yucatan, where she had gone to accept her fate and the will of our Lord Jesus Christ.

That is when something miraculous occurred. Jesus spoke to her saying, "My name is Esu Sananda Kumara" and then sent Thedra down to the Monastery of the Seven Rays in Peru to learn the Kumara wisdom. After five years, Thedra was told to return to the United States where she founded the Association of Sananda and Sanat Kumara at Mt. Shasta in California.

While heading this organization, Thedra channeled many messages from Sananda and taught the Kumara wisdom until her passing in 1992. While in the Yucatan, it is said that Sister Thedra, during the 1960s, was associated with the Kumara.

Sister Thedra, 1900-1992, spent five years at an abbey undergoing intensive spiritual training and initiations. While in South America, she had an experience which changed her in an instant when, as it is told by her, Jesus Christ physically appeared to her and spontaneously cured her of cancer.

He introduced himself to her by his true, name, "Sananda Kumara," thereby revealing his affiliation with the founders of the

Great Solar Brotherhoods. It was by His command that Sister Thedra went to Peru. She eventually left upon being told that her experience there was complete. She then traveled to Mt. Shasta in California and founded the Association of Sananda and Sanat Kumara. A.S.S.K.

You ask, Is There a difference between Jesus and Sananda? Our Lord's name given at birth by his Father Joseph and his beloved mother Mary was Yeshua, thus being of the house of David and the order of Yoseph he would be called Yeshua ben Yoseph. The Roman Emperors placed the name of Jesus upon the sir-name of Yeshua after the Emperor Justinian adopted Christianity as the official faith of Rome and ordered that the sacred books be compiled upon approval of a specially appointed counsel appointed by the Emperor into a recognizable and uniform work titled "The Bible". Prior to this, there never was a Bible per se.

There existed until the time of the Emperor's edict, a selection of many Sacred texts, that were employed in the Sacred Teachings, many of which were copies of what the Greeks had transposed from the original texts in the Libraries of Alexandria, which were originally compiled by Alexander the Great, and were destroyed by Julius Caesar who feared that they might prove dangerous to the rule of a Caesar, an Earthly God.

In addition, it was to keep the knowledge of Alexander's Libraries out of the hands of the Ptolemy's who were said to be descended from his bloodline. (At the time, Caesar had no way of knowing that vast portions of the Library were already in the

Americas, in the Great Universities of the Inca, and in possession of the Mayans.)

Yeshua spent many years in the East after his ascension. The Good Shepherd, upon his appearances to the Apostles after His ascension, told them that He was going to tend to His Father's other sheep; which meant, plainly, that He was continuing upon His sacred journey. As The Ascended One, Yeshua took to Himself the name of Sananda, meaning the Christed One, and Sananda was thus embraced forevermore by the Great Solar Brotherhood. To many of you. this is all new. To others it will be received as a welcome easing of the wall that has so long separated two sides of the same coin. This knowledge is being placed into the ethers and the matrix of thought at this time as it is the time of The Great Awakening and the Christos is already emerging into the new consciousness.

Authority to use the name of Sananda was given to Sister Thedra when Jesus, (Sananda) appeared to her in the Yucatan and cured her instantly of the cancer that had taken over her body. Further, He allowed a picture of his countenance (included herein) to be taken at that time that she might realize the occurrence was more than a dream.

Sanada's Message to her by Sister Thedra: "Sori Sori: Mine hand I have placed upon thine head, and I have given unto thee the authority to use Mine name. Give unto them the name Sananda, by which they shall know Me as the Lord thy God - the Son of God, sent that ye be made to know me, the One sent from out The Inner Temple that there be Light in the world of men. Now it is come when ones which have the will to follow Me shall come to know Me by that name which I commanded thee to give unto the world as Mine New name.

There are many that shall call upon the name of Jesus, yet they will deny the new name as they are want to do. Unto thee I give assurance that I am the One sent that there be Light in the world of men. Now let this be understood, that they that deny Mine New Name, deny Me by any name. So be it I have appointed thee Mine spokesman; I've given unto thee the power and authority to speak for being that which I AM. And I say unto thee Mine child whom I have called forth and anointed thee with the Holy Spirit, thy name shall be as it is now called, Thedra, that name I spoke unto thee from out the ethers, and thou heard Me and accepted that which I gave unto thee; and wherein have I deceived thee? Wherein have I forgotten thee, or left thee alone?"

I say unto thee: "Mine hand is upon thee and I shall sustain thee and you shall come to know that which I have kept for thee. So be it that I have kept thy reward, and at no time shall it be dissipated or scattered, for it is intact. So let this Mine Word suffice them which question thee - let them question, and I shall bear witness for thee. For do I not know Mine servants from the traitors? Do I not reward Mine servants according unto their works or merits? I speak that they might know that I am mindful of Mine servants, that I am not a poor puny priest who has forgotten his servants.

"I say unto them, Mine servants shall be glorified above the crowned heads of the nations which have set themselves apart, and denied Me Mine part of Mine word for they have turned from Me in their conceit and forgetfulness. Now let this go on record as Mine

Word, and I shall give unto them proof, which are of a mind to follow Me. So be it as I have spoken and I am not finished; I shall speak again and again, and I shall rise Mine Voice against them which set foot against Mine servants, and they shall be as ones cast out. So let them ask of Me and I shall enlighten them. So be it I know where of I speak. Be ye as ones blest to accept Me and know Me for that which I AM."

On Saturday, June 13, 1992, at exactly 10.00 PM, at the age of 92, Sister Thedra made her final transition from the comfort of her own bed. When the time arrived, she simply took one small breath and slipped quietly away, without pomp or fanfare.

She left as she had lived: as a humble servant for the greater good. The messages included were given to Sister Thedra before her transition. They are compiled here to give you some idea of the significance of her passing and of the expansion of the work, as she is now free to work unencumbered by the physical limitations and by the pain which has so encumbered her in the past. She has carried on the work here on the Earth plane for the last 50 years because that is where the work was needed. Rest assured that her work now in the higher realms will simply be an extension of that work.

Divine Explanations

Part - I

The following explanations and definitions of terms used by Sananda (Jesus) and the various Sibors were given by Sananda through direct revelation. They are not alphabetical. These explanations should be read over and over.

- - - - - - - - - - -

"My Beloved Sibors please give us plainly the definitions of the following words that there may be no error on our part." - Thedra.

THEMSELF? What is the explanation of your terminology of "Themself" – "themselves"?

"I (Sananda) say unto thee mine beloved, they which would be unto thee a vessel, unto thee a sibor, unto thee teacher, are as ones enlightened of the Father, enlightened of the Father for the light is in them.

They know their parts well, they have their memory, they have mastered the elements, they can do all the things which I do and they take unto "themself" no credit for they have overcome self. They are self-less. Now I say unto them: them which work with thee are the Selfless ones. They ask <u>nothing</u> for "themself." Now while this is true they are as one.

They are within the great brotherhood of the Selfless Ones - the Ones clothed in white. They are as the Royal Assembly - and each unto his own, yet each for all and all for one. Now while in thy world, they (of thy world) are <u>selfish</u> and they are not for the whole - they ask for self and I speak of these as the selfish ones. I speak unto them in terms which they shall come to know and therein is wisdom.

I say that they shall be responsible for "themself" and as a world of me I say they shall be responsible for their society; they "themself" have created it. Now I speak unto thee mine beloved, I say "ye shall be responsible for thyself. He shall be responsible for himself. They as a whole shall be responsible for that which they have created, while thou art responsible unto thyself for thine part - and not held accountable for theirs. Be it so."

BELEIS? "Mighty is the word and great the power thereof. I say unto thee this word carries with it the part of surrender. The word is the release of power - that which is sent forth by the one which asks of the Father His blessing. It is the surrender of the self - the complete surrender of the personal will and letting the Father's will be accomplished in all things through thee. "<u>So</u> <u>be</u> <u>it</u>" - it the accomplishment, the acceptance of the Father's plan."

SELAH? - "The word carries the Seal of Truth - meaning it is without error - no mistake - it is the verification of Truth - not subject to change.

SIBET? – "The Sibet is one which has offered or presented himself as a candidate for the greater learning and for the greater initiation. He comes as an empty vessel that he may be filled. So be it."

SIBOR? - "I am the Sibor of Sibors." - "The Sibor is one which has been illumined of God the Father. He has returned unto the Father purified. He has gone the Royal Road - which means he has overcome death. He has mastered the lower elements - he controls the elements. He can raise the dead - heal the sick - he can create like unto the Father <u>for</u> he has finished his course and won the victory and returned unto the Father the Victor. So be it."

"I am the Sibor of Sibors. I am the first born of Him which hast sent me. Sananda."

LEGIRONS? - "Beloved - I say unto thee: thy opinions and thy dogmas are not the least of these - neither thy creeds. Be it ever that these are great and heavy ones. Now let it be understood that a leg-iron is something which holds thee bound. It is something which holds thee, it keeps thee fast, wherein progress is not possible. Now that progress be made possible, ye shall cut away the legirons.

Knowest thou these bound by legirons? These are to be pitied, they drag them with them, impeding their progress - and they are as ones bound! They are not free - are they? While they serve their sentence - they are as ones bound - they are bond-men - they are bound men - men bound. Now let me say I too am a "bondsman." I came that they may be free. I say I bring unto thee the law which thou shall obey - unto the letter - then I shall give unto thee that which I have kept for thee. Be ye as one prepared for that.

PREPARATION? Now - preparation - what do you mean by "preparation?" "This my beloved is the part which they shall do - the part of preparation is: cleaning thyself of all the opinions, indoctrinations of man. The cup must be emptied. This is thy part, the becoming the "'little child" unopinionated, unscathed and unmarred with or by their doctrines, creeds and crafts. I say the child is unindoctrinated and un-opinonated and is the virgin mind – (yet it does not remain so long in this world). While the little child represents the empty cup - the empty vessel, the Virgin Spirit, it is given unto the child to be one which has come from other realms and to have been in many embodiments, many times: yet the symbol of virginity. Wherein is it said there are none innocent among thee?

WHEREIN I AM? - "Now while thou art yet within the world of men - I am within mine Father's realm, the place wherein there is no darkness, wherein ALL things are known. I say wherein ALL things are known, wherein there is No mystery.

And too - I say when thou hast attained unto thy Royal Road, when thou hast become part of the Royal Assembly, thou shall know as I - thou shall be as I - thou shall be brought into the place wherein I am, for I say unto thee this is attainment. This is the day of Attainment, the day of "becoming," the day of thy salvation. Know ye that this is Mine day - the day for which thou hast waited? I say unto thee: "This is the day of fulfillment. This is Mine Day. Mine Day is come ---"

What is meant by "ALL THE LANDS OF THE EARTH?"- "This I mean, all the lands of the Earth. I have said it, I mean it as I have said it and there is no mystery of or to it."

ALL MANKIND? "This is Mine people - Mine children - Mine flock - Mine Church - Mine brethren - Mine congregation unto whom I shall minister. By Mine own hand shall they be fed and led. These have I came to find. Are not all hu-man beings considered "Man kind"? by thine own standards. Yet all men are not of me."

WHAT DO YOU MEAN - "WILL IT SO"? - "There is power in the "WILL" and the power which they use to create their own torment and confusion is misused energy. Yet they will this - they will it so. Now when ye will to serve me ye give unto me thy undivided attention, the whole heart - thy heart - thine ALL. Yet I say that they which doth attempt to serve me with one hand and the dragon with the other has not willed to serve me. They are not of me - they are not of Mine flock. I say they are either with me or against me. I cannot accept the one hand while they reserve the other for the dragon. They are not wholeheartedly mine.

I make no compromises with the dragon. Mine shall come out from them and surrender unto me themself - their all - without reservation. This is willing it so - for they will the Father's will be done in them, through them, by them. They leave no energy that the dragon may use. They use all their energy to serve me. This is mine word unto thee."

WHAT IS DARKNESS? - "Thine Un-Knowing - thy darkness comes from the fall of man - which one was with God the Father perfect which didst have his memory blanked from him when he didst transgress."

MAYAS VEIL? - "The result of such unknowing - the darkness which man has brought upon himself. The part he has created for himself."

WHAT DOES IT MEAN TO <u>BETRAY</u> <u>ONES</u> <u>SELF</u>? - "This is the sad part for first the 'fall' came from his betrayal - and it hast resulted in the fall - in the veil of Maya - the "illusion" and in thy un-knowing - in thy own darkness."

WHAT OF BETRAYING "HIS OWN TRUST"? - "The plan is all inclusive and includes <u>all</u> - yet there are ones unaware of the "plan" - (and they are not as included in this temple as yet) - no personal reference unto the ones within this temple. Now when one becomes aware of his part, he is given the law and it is provided for his own good and he has the law clearly stated, plainly recorded, and he turns his face away - that he may hide from it. He puts his fingers into his ears that he may not hear it. He gives unto his benefactors the bitter cup and he goes his own willful way.

He has betrayed himself for he shall be caught up short of his course. When he has been given a chance - a "part" within the plan and he has committed himself, he has the responsibility given unto him for that "part" and should he be so foolish as to betray his trust he shall be like unto one which has thrown overboard his <u>own</u> life belt - poor foolish ones!"

WISDOM? - What is meant by the word "Wisdom?" - "Wisdom is that which is light, the knowledge of the law and its proper use. The right use of the law - and this Mine children is Mine part. I come that ye may BECOME wise! Wisdom is thy divine gift - not of man, for man of Earth is foolish indeed - and he is nothing save that which the Father has endowed him. All else is of the world of "illusion" which shall pass into nothingness in the Light which I Am."

WHAT IS THE "PEARL OF GREAT PRICE, THE PRICELESS PEARL? - "That which I offer thee - thy freedom, thy salvation from bondage - thine inheritance in full - Mine word which is not purchased with coin - not bought, neither is it sold. It is the wisdom of which I speak. Mine offer unto thee is without price - it is the 'pearl' - "Mine Pearl."

WHY ARE MIS-SPELLED AND GRAMMATICAL ERRORS USED IN THESE SCRIPTS? - "I am not a conformist. I am not concerned with the letters of man for I am He which has come that they be unbound by their fetters. I say unto them which desireth the letter - unto them the letter.

I say unto thee: be ye as ones free from such bondage. I stand ready to free thee from thy bondage. Unto thee I say - give unto the letter no thought. <u>Hear</u> what I <u>say</u> for I shall say it in many ways as becomes me and serves mine purpose. I say I am no stranger in thine midst. While they know me not, I know them. I see them bowing down before the Golden Calf - and they worship at the shrines which they have set up. (Their own standards of education.) They guild them and bring unto them burnt offerings - yet they close me out.

Be ye not so foolish. <u>Be ye not so foolish</u>! I am come that ye might have Light - Wisdom - Freedom which is the Father's will. While the letter changeth and passeth away - and the letter is not the law - the letter is of no consequence other than to cause thee to see the "Word." The word is the power which shall provoke thine mind into action and thy mind shall be free from the letter. See what is meant within the Word, and let thine mind be staid on <u>me</u> - the Light, the Way - Truth and Wisdom."

"I am He which hast come - that ye be free: forever free. I am Sananda - Son of God. Once known as the Nazarine, He which was born of Mary, Ward of Joseph.

Recorded by Thedra

Part - 2

THE WHITE BROTHERHOOD AND THE EMERALD CROSS.

THE MANY QUESTIONS ABOUT THE WHITE BROTHERHOOD AND THE ORDER OF THE EMERALD CROSS MAY BE EXPLAINED IN A FEW SIMPLE WORDS.

ONE HAS TO EARN THE RIGHT TO BECOME A MEMBER - EITHER IN THIS LIFE OR OTHERS BEFORE OR AFTER - NONE ENTER UNPREPARED.

THE WHITE BROTHERHOOD - or - THE ROYAL ASSEMBLY is of the Realms of Light---not of Earth. The Ascended Masters have proven themself in the school of Earth (THE SCHOOL FOR GODS) who have trodden the path of INITIATION - overcome the trials and temptations of the mundane world - who have gained their freedom and ascended as the Lord Jesus Christ (Sananda). They have gone the ROYAL ROAD.

Knowing the path of the Initiate -- and its pitfalls -- and sorrow, they extend a hand in Fellowship - LOVE and WISDOM - NEVER depriving the candidate an opportunity to learn his lessons well -- for this is His salvation -- for this do they proffer their hand, NOT to do our part for us, but rather that we become strong and free by our own strength.

The Royal Assembly or the White Brotherhood have known all of the heartaches, the longing, crucifications, temptations and JOYS of the aspirant -- the candidate -- the Master -- the Sibor -- herein lies their strength, their understanding, their great love for us on the path.

Their love and understanding knows no bounds. They give help when necessary for our progress. They also withhold it wisely - should it deprive us of our lessons. The candidate on the path of initiation shall become self-responsible for all his actions -- all the energy allotted him throughout his whole EARTHLY existence - and make atonement for all his misused energy, for therein is his salvation.

There is no one else which will ever make this atonement for us (the candidate) on the path of unfoldment. While the host of "WHITE BROTHERS" Brothers of LIGHT are ready to assist, the candidate shall (MUST) put forth every effort to overcome all the forces of darkness which would deter his progress and earn for himself his freedom from BONDAGE.

THE EMERALD CROSS

THE EMERALD CROSS is a company – and an order of beings who work within the Brotherhood of MAN - and the Fatherhood of God - for the good of all mankind --- And at the head of this group is one known as MOTHER SARAH, the personification of love -- embodiment of all MOTHERS. That is: the LOVE of God made Manifest - in MOTHERS. The blessed Mother Sarah is the head of this Order of the Emerald Cross. And when one earns the Divine right and privileges to associate themselves with this Order, it is the joy of all the Orders - and Brothers of Light. I speak for the Order - for I am known as Merseda. (As told to Sister Thedra of the Order of the Emerald Cross).

COMANCHE - which is the porter at the door - which doth keep out the unworthy, the unjust, the unclean. The Door Keeper - the one responsible for the Temple Gate.

<u>BITTER</u> <u>CUP</u> - that which you would not like to partake of - that which poisons thee, that which is not good, that which torments thee - that which ye have given unto thy brother to torment him which returns unto thee as a boomerang to torment thee - which ye shall receive multiplied - which has accumulated in its swift flight. I say prepare not for thyself the bitter cup for ye shall drink of the portion which thou doth prepare for thy brother. Be ye not foolish - make it not bitter.

<u>BLEST</u> <u>OF</u> <u>MINE</u> <u>BEING</u> - I have given of Mine self that Mine beloved has being.

<u>BLEST</u> <u>OF</u> <u>MINE</u> <u>PRESENCE</u> - Have I not gone the long way? I have gone out from Mine place of abode that I might bring light unto the Earth that she might be lifted up - that the children thereof might be delivered of all bondage - that they might return unto the place from whence they went out. And have I not come unto thee many times that this be accomplished? Have I not done all which has been given unto me to do? Wherein have I failed thee? Have I not done all that I have come to do? - While it is not as yet finished, I shall not fail. My mission shall be finished ere I return unto Mine abiding place. Shall I not be unto the true and shall I not return the Victor?

<u>GAVE</u> <u>OF</u> <u>HIMSELF</u> - Did I not give of Mine Self - hast thou? Have I not been true unto Mine trust? Have I asked aught for Myself? Have I not done that which I have promised? Have I not given Mine All? Have I not come on a Sacrificial Mission? What more have I to give - other than myself?

<u>PORE</u> - The physical body - vehicle which thou dost use.

<u>INITIATION</u> - Thy preparation for the inner temple. Each step is an initiation. One step at a time - the overcoming of self - the world - the becoming that which I am.

<u>COSMOS</u> - That which is unseen throughout many universes by thy eyes. Great is the expanse of the Father's Kingdom and the total thereof is referred to as "throughout the Cosmos."

<u>LORD'S</u> <u>STRANGE</u> <u>ACT</u> - This I shall reveal in Mine own time.

<u>WALK</u> <u>WHICH</u> <u>WAY</u> <u>THY</u> <u>CROWN</u> <u>TILTS</u> <u>NOT</u> - as a Son of God. Do honor unto thy Father Mother God - and thou shall be as one which has the Royal Raiment upon thine shoulders - and ye shall wear it in honor and with dignity.

<u>WHEN</u> <u>IT</u> <u>SAYS</u> <u>IT</u> <u>IS</u> <u>RECORDED</u> - <u>WHEREIN</u> <u>IS</u> <u>IT</u> <u>RECORDED</u>? - In the secret place - in the eth - and within the inner temple - and wherein thou art are many things recorded - which I do speak of. Ye shall see these recordings when thou doth enter into the secret place of Mine abode. I say ye shall read the records wherein are written the records of all thy travels from the time ye left the Father Mother God until thine return unto him.

<u>WHAT</u> <u>IS</u> <u>MICHAEL'S</u> <u>FLAMING</u> <u>SWORD</u>? - "The "Sword of Truth and justice."

Recorded by Sister Thedra

Other Books by TNT Publishing

Who am I and Why Am I here?

The Significance of Existence

Death and the Incredible Life After

Fear of Death Removed

Paradise Regained

Spiritual Laws Revealed

Unseen Forces

Too Good to Be True

The Truth of Life in the Spirit World

He Who Has Ears

The Great Awakening, Volumes I thru VII

The Great Awakening, Volume VIII,
THE WHITE STAR OF THE EAST

The Great Awakening, Volume IX,
I THE LORD GOD SAY UNTO THEM

The Great Awakening, Volume X,
MINE INTERCOM MESSAGES FROM THE REALMS OF LIGHT

The Great Awakening, Volume XI,
THE BOOK OF THE LORD

The Great Awakening, Volume XII thru XV,
TEMPLE TEACHINGS FROM THE HIGHER REALMS

Transfiguration Volumes I thru Volume VIII

Contact us at

Email: goldtown11@gmail.com

Web: https://www.whoamiandwhyamihere.com/

www.ingramcontent.com/pod-product-compliance
Lightning Source LLC
LaVergne TN
LVHW051547070426
835507LV00021B/2443